S0-ABC-402

www.wadsworth.com

www.wadsworth.com is the World Wide Web site for Wadsworth and is your direct source to dozens of online resources.

At *www.wadsworth.com* you can find out about supplements, demonstration software, and student resources. You can also send email to many of our authors and preview new publications and exciting new technologies.

www.wadsworth.com
Changing the way the world learns®

A Primer of California Politics

Second Edition

LAWRENCE G. BREWSTER
University of San Francisco

GENIE N. L. STOWERS
San Francisco State University

THOMSON
™
WADSWORTH

Australia • Canada • Mexico • Singapore • Spain
United Kingdom • United States

Publisher: Clark Baxter
Executive Editor: David Tatom
Development Editor: Scott Spoolman
Editorial Assistant: Reena Thomas
Technology Project Manager:
   Melinda Newfarmer
Marketing Manager: Janise Fry
Marketing Assistant: Mary Ho
Advertising Project Manager:
   Nathaniel Bergson-Michelson
Project Manager, Editorial Production:
   Ray Crawford

Print/Media Buyer: Jessica Reed
Permissions Editor: Sarah Harkrader
Production Service: G & S Typesetters, Inc.
Text Designer: G & S Typesetters, Inc.
Copy Editor: Chris Sabooni
Illustrator: G & S Typesetters, Inc.
Cover Designer: Brian Salisbury
Cover Image: AP/ Wide World Photos
Cover Printer: Webcom Limited
Compositor: G & S Typesetters, Inc.
Printer: Webcom Limited

Library of Congress Control Number:
2003106023
ISBN 0-534-61839-1

Wadsworth / Thomson Learning
10 Davis Drive
Belmont, CA 94002-3098
USA

**For more information about our products,
contact us at:**
**Thomson Learning Academic
Resource Center
1-800-423-0563**

Asia
Thomson Learning
5 Shenton Way #01-01
UIC Building
Singapore 068808

Australia/New Zealand
Thomson Learning
102 Dodds Street
Southbank, Victoria 3006
Australia

Canada
Nelson
1120 Birchmount Road
Toronto, Ontario M1K 5G4
Canada

Europe/Middle East/Africa
Thomson Learning
High Holborn House
50/51 Bedford Row
London WC1R 4LR
United Kingdom

To Sean, Noreen, Gabriela, and Marissa

Contents

Preface

Californians face many challenges in the 21st century. The newly reelected governor, Gray Davis, and the legislature must close a projected budget deficit of $21 billion. The state's economy is in a slump, with no immediate signs of recovery. The schools continue to struggle to meet the needs of a very diverse student population, as the teachers remain underpaid. Clogged highways, pollution, inadequate water supplies, relatively high crime rates, and heightened tensions between ethnic and racial groups, as well as a growing number of hate crimes, are some of the negative side-effects of rapid growth and overpopulation. At the same time, California remains a land of promise and hope for peoples of all color, origin, and lifestyle. It is rich in natural resources and continues to attract creative and educated people emboldened with the entrepreneurial spirit.

One of the most important and troubling developments in California is the loss of trust in the government's ability to solve the state's problems. In the 2002 gubernatorial election, neither the incumbent Gray Davis nor his Republican challenger, Bill Simon, garnered much voter enthusiasm or trust. Record low voter turnout, and the fact that the "winner," Gray Davis, received less than 50 percent of the vote suggests that the voters (and nonvoters, for that matter) have little confidence in their elected officials. Californians see gridlock and interest group politics in Sacramento much as they do in Washington. Evidence of their dissatisfaction with politics as usual is the frequent use of the initiative process, including passage of Proposition 140 (1990), which limits elected officials' terms in office, and Proposition 187 (1994), which denies services to illegal immigrants. Repeated attempts to reform state and local governments have failed largely because power brokers have a vested interest in the status quo and because the public chooses to remain outside the political process. Governor Gray Davis's opponent in the 2002 election criticized him for spending so much of his time fund-raising, and catering to special interests—public opinion polls showed that a majority of voters also thought Davis spent too much time on raising unprecedented campaign dollars.

This is an exciting time to study California politics. The state is the dominant economic and political power in the nation—even though George W. Bush was elected president without carrying the state. It remains a trendsetter in social movements and serves as a laboratory for other states in finding solutions to the problems of today and the future. In the process, it also serves as a lightning rod in the more controversial policy arenas such as affirmative action and immigration.

The state is rich in its diversity of cultures, languages, lifestyles, and geography. This richness is one reason California politics is so unpredictable and, in turn, so interesting. It also is a place in desperate need of informed and active citizenship if it is to remain the Golden State and not become, in the words of novelist Christopher Isherwood, a "tragic place." Every one of its citizens has an obligation to become educated in California politics so that, as informed citizens, they may make a difference in the state's future. We think the rediscovery of citizenship is at least as important as a reinvention of government.

A Primer of California Politics is designed as a companion book to an American Government textbook. It delivers the essential information for the least cost in time and money to students. Written in everyday language, the first two chapters place students within a historical and policy context to assist them in understanding the dynamics of California politics. Every chapter, even those that discuss the nuts and bolts of California government, attempt to make very personal and vivid the inner workings of government so as to reach even those students who feel themselves to be alienated from the body politic.

The book is unique to other California government textbooks in some other important ways. We think students are more likely to care about California politics if they are first introduced to the many challenges and possibilities that exist in this truly amazing state. The first two chapters accomplish this by bringing the California political, social, and economic landscape alive. *A Primer of California Politics* considers the important public policy issues confronting the state in the 21st century.

Integrated into the chapters are the important structural differences between the federal and California governments. This is particularly useful considering most students study American government at about the same time they are required to learn about California government. Each chapter includes a special feature entitled "A Closer Look," two or more boxes per chapter that provide students with the opportunity to explore via the Internet and other modes particular questions or issues posed to them. We think this unique feature will challenge students to investigate in greater detail important aspects of California policy and politics.

We think local government is given too little attention in most other text-books. We find students know very little about the government that is closest to them and the one that they are most likely to interact with on a daily basis. Our book ends with a very thorough and, we think, lively discussion of local government in California.

Visually, the text will provide guidance to students reading through extensive use of subtitles, graphic displays of data, suggested governmental reforms to stimulate student debate, and suggested readings. The writing is brisk, readable, and, we hope, student-friendly.

We wish to thank the several people who made this book possible. We are grateful to the following reviewers for their insightful comments and suggestions:

- John M. Dineen, California State University–Sacramento
- Jeanne L. Gilkey, San Jose State University
- Richard L. Harris, California State University–Monterey Bay
- Richard D. Hughes, California State University–Sacramento
- Sarbjit Johal, Fresno City College
- John D. Kay, Santa Barbara City College
- Jack Kornblau, City College of San Francisco
- Marcelo C. Ramos, Golden Gate University

We thank Scott Spoolman for his invaluable editorial feedback. The book is very much better for his insight and assistance. Likewise, we are indebted to Mark Nichol for his help in formatting the text and graphics, and for his editing. April Eleyce Latragna did an excellent job of designing many of the tables, graphs, and figures.

Finally, we wish to thank those closest to us—Noreen, Sean, Butch, Marissa, and Gabriela. Without their love and support, this and all other accomplishments would have little meaning for us.

Lawrence G. Brewster
Genie N. L. Stowers

A Primer of California Politics

1

California's Crossroads

We begin with the story of Frances Esquibel Tywoniak, the daughter of an immigrant father from northern Mexico, and herself an immigrant to California from New Mexico. In her own words, she captures what it was like growing up as an immigrant in California during the 1930s, 1940s, and 1950s.

We lived in a Spanish-speaking world. For the most part, we spoke Spanish on a daily basis. My father especially insisted on this and was very conscious of our use of language. The Great Depression worsened as the thirties progressed, and my father decided to go to California in search of economic opportunities. My parents wanted a good life for us, and that meant having enough to eat and a decent place to live. A good life to them also meant having some level of economic self-sufficiency. Home ownership remained a goal.

We eventually migrated to the Tagus Ranch, which was situated between Visalia and Tulare, still in the San Joaquin Valley. I was now about seven years old. I remember vividly our housing situation. It was a farm-labor camp, and families were designated to live in particular sections identified by the coloring of the frame shacks. I don't know if those distinctions had anything to do with race or ethnicity, even though overall it was quite a mixed community of people: Mexicans, a few African Americans, and many whites—the so-called Okies and Arkies.

I existed in two worlds. . . . On one side there was the sphere of experiences at school; these experiences had little, if anything, to do with my real life. Alongside that sphere but apart from it was what I believed was actually real about me, my family. One additional source of alienation had to do with language and how it affected my relationship to my parents. I was becoming more proficient in English, while Spanish remained our language at home.

By the time I was about eight or nine, I started being conscious of the fact that these worlds didn't exist in a state of harmony. The more my school world became an English-speaking one, the more I resented having to speak Spanish at home. . . . By then, if Anglos saw my parents as foreigners, I, in my own way, was beginning to do the same, certainly with respect to school.

We moved to Visalia in 1941. Visalia represented my introduction to barrio life. We were no longer in company-owned housing; we were renters. Visalia was a town rather than a big city, but it certainly had separate and different residential areas. I understood, in a very general way, that there were two sides of town: the Anglo side and the Mexican side.

This period coincided with the pachuco era, which was especially associated with the Los Angeles area. This was the period of the zoot-suit riots in 1943. I didn't care for them [pachucos and pachucas]. My fears and rejection of the pachucas reflected the fact that the barrio was not some stereotypical homogeneous community. There were differences and divisions. There were tensions and animosities. We all came from different places. It wasn't as if we were all one people.

My entering high school in 1945 coincided with our move out of the barrio. This was symbolic for me. My parents, after having worked hard for several years in California, had been able to save enough money to purchase or at least make a down payment on a house. Visalia Union High was ethnically mixed but there was also ethnic separation. Mexicans were largely concentrated in non-college-track courses, while Anglos and a few Mexicans like myself were in the better classes.

My high school years only furthered my sense that I was living in two distinct worlds. I knew that I wanted to succeed in high school. To achieve something better for myself, I knew I had to compete in a world that was really a world of los americanos. And I did. [Excerpted from Frances Esquibel Tywoniak and Mario T. Garcia, *Migrant Daughter: Coming of Age as a Mexican American Woman* (Berkeley, CA: University of California Press.) Copyright © 1999 by The Regents of the University of California. Used with permission.]

She did indeed. Frances was awarded a scholarship to UC Berkeley, graduating in 1953. There she met and married Ed Tywoniak, a Polish American, thereby bridging still another culture. She went on to a successful career as a teacher and school administrator.

THE LURE OF THE CALIFORNIA DREAM

Frances's story is one of the millions of immigrant stories that make up the rich tapestry of California life and its history. California is a land of immigrants. California's place as the fifth-largest economy in the world is in large measure due to the hard work, creativity, intelligence, and sheer will of immigrants. They tilled the land, picked the crops, worked in the factories, built the railroad, and helped to create Silicon Valley, and they introduced us to new foods, music, art, and languages.

The promise of jobs attracted people like Frances's parents from every part of the country, and the world. Pursuit of the California Dream has taken different forms and meanings for those who migrated to this great land, but all felt they would find happiness and the good life. Allow us to tell one more story about a family that migrated to California in search of a fresh start. This story is of a more personal nature, and one that illustrates what it must have been like for so many young people when they first arrived in the Golden State. This story also speaks to the changed environment of California since that boy first arrived by train in 1927. This is the story of James R. Brewster.

> My father was a very good farmer in North Western Iowa near the town of Sheldon. One morning, as he was dressing to do the morning chores at 4:30 am, he fell back on the bed and told my mother he could not see. He was having the first of a series of strokes. He was 34 years of age. After his second or third stroke, my mother knew we could no longer stay on the farm. We had a farm sale that included our stock, equipment, etc. With six children, the youngest child two years old, myself being 12, the third oldest, and an invalid husband, we were ready to leave for California where my mother's parents lived.
>
> It was February 1927 when my uncle took us into Sheldon during a blizzard on a bobsled pulled by a team of horses. This was the only way we could travel in the snowstorm. We boarded a train that took us to Omaha, Nebraska, where we transferred to a Union Pacific train to Pomona, California. Pomona was a small town about 35 miles east of Los Angeles. While waiting in Omaha, my sister and I rode an elevator up and down. We had never experienced inside plumbing or electricity, let alone an elevator! While riding from Omaha to Pomona in coach seats for four days, we never left the train. Finally, we stepped off the train on a beautiful February morning. The palm trees along the tracks were glistening in the sun, the San Gabriel mountain range 20 or so miles north with Mt. Baldy at 10,000 feet were covered in snow. Standing on the green grass at the station fresh from a blizzard, I developed a deep and profound love for California that is just as profound seventy-five years later.
>
> Today, however, California is a different place. Pomona in 1927 had a population of approximately 19,000, while today it is around 200,000. Pomona Valley was an agricultural area with citrus groves, dairy farms, chicken hatcheries and cattle ranches in the hills. Today, it is a valley filled

A Closer Look

As you read Frances's or James's story, think about your own life. What are your family roots? What was your neighborhood like growing up? Are you a native Californian, or did you migrate from another state or country? If so, how have you experienced California? Do you relate to Frances's story? If you are a native Californian, interview your parents, a fellow student, or neighbor who is from another state or country. Ask about their experiences as immigrants.

with housing, strip malls, and industry. The Santa Ana River flowed full with clean mountain water, the canyons in the San Gabriels also sent creek water down to the valley and the water table came to the surface near the hills to the south in the form of artesian water, which formed a creek called Chino Creek that flowed in the Santa Ana River. Over time, with demand for water to serve the population and industrial growth, the artesian water disappeared and so did Chino Creek. (Excerpted from an unpublished letter sent to Lawrence Brewster, written by his father.)

For many, like Frances and James, the dream of a good life came true, while others are still waiting, hoping.

California has reinvented itself in the past and is doing so again today. A dramatic combination of demographic shifts, new technologies, economic restructuring, population growth, environmental challenges, and changes in social attitudes foreshadows a different California in the 21st century. California is at a crossroads; it remains to be seen which way it will go. The same could be said of California in the 19th and 20th centuries and for similar reasons. Rapid population growth, environmental destruction, integration of newly arrived immigrants, calls for political reform, and the creation of vast new wealth are familiar themes in the history of this amazing state.

California began as a legend in 16th century Spain, when it was mythologized as "a fantastic island 'very near terrestrial paradise,' ruled by the goddess Califia and inhabited by Amazons. Their arms are all of gold as is the harness of the wild beats they ride. In all the island there is no other metal."[1]

While we know California is neither an island, nor a land of only gold, nor even Amazons, we do know that certainly since the early days in 1849 when gold was discovered, it has attracted millions of people in search of the good life—however they may have envisioned it.

The question is, has the promised "good life," or the California Dream, become more myth than reality? If the California Dream is measured only in economic success, then one might argue that California remains a place of promise. There is little question that fortunes are made every day in the entertainment, technology, and bioengineering fields—a kind of second gold rush. But, if we talk in terms of the environment, population explosion, transporta-

---

BOX 1.1   At a Crossroads: Which Way California?

An environmental scan of California conducted by the Irvine Foundation in 2000 identified five major issues that will challenge California in the 21st century. They are

- Snowballing ethnic, racial, and cultural diversity. California will have no ethnic majority until 2040, when Latinos will constitute 50 percent of the population. During the next 30 years, more than one in every three American immigrants is expected to live in California.

- Population growth that promises to catapult us from 34 million to 45 million in 20 years.

- A disturbing disengagement from civic participation, especially among young people. In the 1996 presidential election, only 31 percent of eligible voters between the ages of 18 and 24 voted. There is a widening mistrust of institutions and an expanding gulf between citizen and government.

- A disaffection from state and local politics. In 1999, 47 percent of the respondents in a statewide poll could not name the governor of the state of California.

- The challenge of harnessing technology for public benefit to avoid growing economic disparities and deepening isolation in a high-tech world.

SOURCE: Dennis Collins, President and CEO of the James Irvine Foundation, in a speech delivered to the Commonwealth Club of California, San Francisco, September 20, 2000.

---

tion, education, and related quality of life issues, the Golden State appears more tarnished. A review of California history reveals these issues are not unique to California in the early 21st century.

California's story is a fascinating one. The new economy is reminiscent of the days when thousands rushed to mine for gold, and others made fortunes selling clothing, housing, mining equipment, and other goods and services to the miners. The dot-comers fueled the boom of the 1990s, creating vast fortunes for those lucky enough to cash in before the bust hit in 2000.

The 1849 gold rush transformed California almost overnight from a sleepy, pastoral spot at the far end of the continent into the most populated and richest state in the Union. However, concerns about the environment, crime, housing costs, and other quality of life issues concerned Californians in the heady days of the gold rush, just as they are on our minds today (see Box 1.1). Racial and ethnic tensions and violence date back to when American settlers first took California from Mexico and when Native Americans were devastated by their contact with Europeans, their culture, and their diseases.

A study of California politics necessarily begins with a look backward. Our lives are influenced by decisions that were made by political and economic leaders of earlier generations. Those earlier decisions must be understood in the context of the social, economic, and political conditions of their era, just as we need to understand the context of today's decisions.

BEFORE STATEHOOD: PRE-1848 HISTORY

In the earliest days of American history, California was a distant outpost to early America. Native Americans and Mexicans (known as Californios) first populated California. It is estimated that 300,000 Native Americans, made up of more than 20 language groups and 100 dialects, lived conflict-free in California before Europeans arrived. The Native Americans living in this part of the country supported themselves largely by fishing, agriculture, and foraging. Native Americans living on the Pacific Coast did not have warriors, nor did they have a tradition of warfare.[2] This changed when with the arrival of Europeans in the early 1500s.[3]

Spanish explorers first entered the territory in the mid-1500s. Priests set up missions in the 1770s, using Indian converts as laborers. Spanish and Mexican settlers, called *Californios,* soon followed, carving out huge ranches worked by American Indian slaves. These settlers brought with them Christianity, European ideas about how Native Americans should live, and diseases such as smallpox and measles that took a terrible toll on the native population. Devastated by the diseases and the lifestyles imported by Europeans, more than half of the 300,000 Native Americans had died by 1841.[4]

California became a part of the Spanish Empire in the early 1500s when Spain conquered Mexico. Even in the state's early history, people from around the world were drawn to California. Russian and British trappers explored its coast in search of sea otter pelts. Fearing takeover by these early explorers, the Spanish government established in the mid-1500s permanent settlements, including Catholic missions, presidios (military garrisons), and, later, small Spanish-styled villages known as pueblos.

After it won independence from Spain in 1821, the Mexican government secularized the missions and appropriated their lands. The land was divided between the Native Americans who lived and worked at the missions (known as mission Indians) and new settlers who were attracted by the promise of land grants.

Most mission Indians lost their land to corrupt administrators and to the new settlers who migrated from across the country. These new settlers became increasingly disaffected with the ineffectual and remote government in Mexico City. At the same time, the U.S. government's desire to control all the territory up to the Pacific grew.

About the time the United States admitted Texas into the Union in 1845, Americans were also showing greater interest in California. American traders, and later merchants, established stores, imported merchandise, and developed a profitable trade with the Mexicans and Native Americans. Eventually, pioneering farmers entered California from the East by land and settled in the Sacramento Valley, establishing roots in the Golden State. A growing number of these early settlers began to dream about bringing California into the Union.

The United States had already severed diplomatic relations with Mexico over Texas. James K. Polk was elected President largely on his pledge to annex Texas. Shortly after his election, Texas became a state in December 1845. Once

Texas was admitted to statehood, Polk offered to buy California from Mexico, without success. While efforts to purchase the territory were under way, a few settlers in northern California plotted to overthrow the Californios—they were never a strong military force—and take California from Mexico. The Bear Flag Revolt was nothing more than a few settlers seizing control of the town of Sonoma in 1845 and hoisting a flag with a crudely drawn bear, declaring California as the "Bear Flag Republic." It was one of the shortest-lived republics in history, but the bear and the words "California Republic" remain today on the state flag.

STATEHOOD

The United States declared war on Mexico in May 1846. In short order, U.S. troops occupied all the presidios, and by 1847 they had seized Mexico City. The treaty ending the Mexican-American War required Mexico to cede a huge area of land to the United States, including California. Soon after the treaty was signed, gold was discovered in northern California. In the early 1840s, before the gold rush, California was little more than a vast area of land consisting of a few small towns, a handful of crumbling Spanish missions, and vast herds of cattle owned by the Californios.

More than 90,000 people flooded the state in the two years following the discovery of gold. The gold rush constituted the largest mass migration in American history. Among the many people who joined the rush for gold were Chinese immigrants, who had success in mining until the California legislature passed in 1850 a foreign miners tax designed to exclude the Chinese—and Mexicans—from mining. This was one of the first laws passed by the newly formed state legislature. Earlier in that same year, California was admitted to the Union as a non-slave state.

It took only 43 days to draft California's first constitution. Why did it take so little time? Because Congress had refused more than once to grant California territorial status, the new California officials felt they had to move quickly to draft a state constitution. Congress was reluctant to grant territorial status to California because they were divided over the delicate issue of slave versus free soil states. However, by the summer of 1849, the situation had become critical as the population swelled and the Mexican civil law in place at the time was no longer functioning effectively.[5]

Pat Ooley, a graduate student of public history at the University of California at Santa Barbara and archive researcher for the Secretary of State's California State Archives, writes:

> President of the United States Zachary Taylor suggested a solution for California: frame a constitution and petition Congress directly for immediate statehood when it next convened. That is what California did. In just nine months (June 1849 to March 1850), California elected delegates to a constitutional convention; framed, distributed, and ratified a

constitution; and elected a first legislature, which then elected two Senators to Congress.[6]

This first state constitution, which lasted 30 years, borrowed heavily from the U.S. Constitution as well as from the state constitutions of Iowa and New York. It was relatively short and woefully inadequate. It imposed few controls on the legislature, failed to address state spending, and ignored railroad interests' corrupting influences. An ineffectual government, controlled by special interests at a time when California's economy was in a severe slump, combined to make voters angry. In 1877, the Workingman's Party, under the leadership of Denis Kearney, called for a reform of the constitution. In the same year, the voters approved a proposal for a constitutional convention. The delegates worked for five months to create the longest state constitution of its day. The proverbial pendulum swung to the other extreme in an effort to correct the omissions in the first constitution.

California's tremendous growth after the discovery of gold encouraged the national goal of building a transcontinental railroad. During the Civil War, despite issues of sectionalism, costs, and engineering challenges, the Union adopted the project as a national necessity. In 1862, President Lincoln signed the Pacific Railroad Act, which authorized the Central Pacific Railroad to build east from Sacramento and the Union Pacific Railroad to build west from the Missouri River.

Four California merchants underwrote the new railroad: Leland Stanford, Charles Crocker, Mark Hopkins, and Collis Huntington—the so-called Big Four. They were merchants who helped to finance the Central and Southern Pacific Railroads. The project began early in 1863 at Front and K Streets in Sacramento. Due in great part to the Mexican and Chinese laborers, the Central Pacific and Union Pacific Railroads joined at Promontory Summit, Utah, on May 10, 1869. California was now linked to the rest of the nation.

THE PROGRESSIVE MOVEMENT

Contemporary California is largely a product of developments that took place between 1880 and 1920. In particular, urbanization, industrialization, and immigration impacted the state in both beneficial and destructive ways. The historian Arthur Mann writes that modernization cost America in the form of "social dislocation, moral confusion, and human suffering. Why, asked an observer, must abysmal poverty accompany economic growth? The response to that and other paradoxes deriving from the rapid transformation of a commercial-agricultural society was the Progressive movement."[7]

Powerful individuals and trusts, particularly the railroads, virtually owned the state.[8] Their abuses of power were uncovered by crusading journalists known as "muckrakers" who were committed to social justice through their writing. Simultaneously, the short-lived Populist Party and a small, but thriving, Socialist community lay the groundwork for the eventually far more successful Progressive Movement.

Calls for political reform in the mid-1870s centered on the need to restrict the powers of state and local legislators, and government regulation of monopolies. The men and women who fought for social justice and who were optimistic that California could become an even greater state without political corruption and monopolistic powers were instrumental in helping the Progressives to change the political, social, and economic landscape of California. Populist proposals such as ballot reform, initiative, referendum, recall, direct primaries, and unemployment relief have long since been enacted into law.

Populists and Progressives distrusted politics and political leadership. They staked their reform efforts on transference of political power to the people. This was the appeal of direct legislation in the form of the initiative and referendum. These reformers and their general distrust of political leadership contributed to a weakening of political parties in California. California politics to this day places an emphasis on the individual, rather than on the political party.[9]

California's constitution has been revised many times since it was adopted in 1879. Unlike the U.S. Constitution, its original model, the state constitution provides details for running the government, including formulating and administering public policy. With 80,000 words, the California constitution is ten times the length of the U.S. Constitution. It is the world's third-longest constitution.

It has been amended nearly 500 times; the U.S. Constitution has only 27 amendments. The state constitution, including most of its amendments, involves policy matters more commonly left to simple legislative action. The constitution's specificity creates a potential problem. While laws that are passed by the legislature are relatively easy to change if necessary, the same cannot be said for constitutional amendments. Revisions to the constitution require a constitutional convention, a referendum, or an initiative.

In 1962, a commission was formed to review the constitution and to recommend changes to modernize and streamline the document. Seven years later it recommended that many ambiguities, dated language, and unnecessary details be deleted. If all of their suggestions had been adopted, the constitution's length would have been halved. Over a ten-year period, the legislature and the voters accepted three-fourths of the proposed changes. Still, each newly passed initiative increases the document's length. Professor Jeffrey Chapman, Director of Public Affairs at the University of Southern California, sums up the California constitution best when he describes it as "the perfect example of what a constitution ought *not* to be."[10]

Earlier, we wrote about the pre-Progressive generation that fought for political and economic reform in the 1880s and 1890s. Although they enjoyed a few legislative victories, more importantly, they awakened the democratic conscience that changed profoundly the political landscape of America between 1900 and 1920. The Progressive Movement, which actually consisted of several different movements, rested on definable, widely shared, unifying principles.

They were the spirit of antimonopoly, the belief in social cohesion, and the belief in organization and efficiency.

In other words, the Progressives were opposed to concentrated power and wanted wealth to be more evenly distributed across the social spectrum. They believed that social relationships were important, and that individuals depended upon society for their well being. Alan Brinkley, the Allan Nevins Professor of History at Columbia University, points out that the Progressives had confidence in "intelligent social organization and rational procedures for guiding social and economic life."[11]

Progressives feared concentrated power. They worked to curb the economic and political excesses of industrial titans and political bosses. While Progressives did not always agree on specific interventions, they generally believed that government alone could effectively counter the powerful private interests that, in their view, threatened the nation.[12]

The Progressives' first goal was to reform government—beginning with political parties, which they believed had become corrupt, undemocratic, and reactionary. They recommended breaking the stranglehold of parties by allowing citizens to express their desires directly at the polls, bypassing the parties and politicians. They also suggested that power could be placed in the hands of nonpartisan, non-elective officials such as appointed agency directors and regulators.

At this time in California history, the state and local governments were relatively powerless compared with states outside of the West. Progressive Hiram Johnson and other California reformers exploited this weakness and moved quickly and decisively to embrace reforms such as the initiative, the referendum, the recall, and the direct primary, which will be discussed in Chapter 4.

Political parties were not eliminated from American political life as a result of the reforms promoted by the Progressives. Over time, however, political parties no longer played a central role in politics.

We face many of the same issues in the 21st century that the Progressives confronted at the turn of the last century. The Progressives in their day had to make hard choices among differing immigration policies, economic policies, social policies, and government reforms in an effort to address the social dislocation, inequities, and injustices brought on by industrialization and urbanization. Many of these same conditions exist today, and many of the same policy issues make up today's political agenda. How well did the Progressives respond to their challenges? This question is still debated by historians. How well will we choose in our policy-making is an even more daunting question.

THE CALIFORNIA BOOM

More than a million families from Oklahoma, Texas, Arkansas, and Missouri fled to California during the Great Depression of the 1930s and early 1940s. Although droughts and dust storms were not new to the Plains states, the terrible "dust bowl" of the early 1930s was unprecedented in its severity. Many of those who migrated from Oklahoma (the so-called Okies) and Texas were victims of the dust bowl, having lost their farms or other jobs. Those who migrated from Arkansas (the so-called Arkies) and Missouri were not affected so much by the drought as they were victims of large-scale agribusinesses. More Americans followed in the post–World War II years. Many of the soldiers and sailors who experienced the sunshine and beauty of California decided to settle in the Golden State after the war.

How did Californians fare during the depression years? The national economic downturn of the early 1930s hit California hard, leaving many to experience deprivation similar to that of other Americans. James N. Gregory, Professor of History at the University of California, Berkeley, notes, "business failure and unemployment had soared, leaving more than 700,000 Californians, 29 percent of the work force, jobless by early 1933."[13] Gregory concludes, however, that California was not as vulnerable as most other states because of its diverse economy.[14]

It was not easy finding work in California, but the state did offer one of the country's most generous unemployment relief programs. Gregory notes, "after 1933 the California State Relief Administration saw to it that eligible unemployed residents received relief checks averaging about $40 a month for a family of four. That was at least double what most Southwestern states paid in unemployment relief."[15]

Like most states, California pulled out of the Great Depression at the beginning of World War II. Almost overnight, California industry provided military equipment, food, and other products for the American war effort. People moved from all over the country to work in California. The war created a high demand for food. Mexicans—known as "braceros"—were brought into the state to satisfy the need for cheap farm labor.[16]

The end of World War II marked the beginning of an amazing chapter in California history. A migration nearly as large as that of 1849 occurred during and immediately following the war, including large numbers of Blacks— resulting in racial tension and bias not unlike that experienced in the South. Blacks for the first time joined Asians and Hispanics as a sizable minority group in southern California, particularly Los Angeles.

The migration occurred, in part, as a result of the growing defense industry. The demand for workers was insatiable.[17] As a result of the defense buildup, California's unemployment rate, still 14 percent in early 1940, plummeted. By mid-1942, joblessness was but a bitter memory in most parts of the state. In the words of James Gregory, "California during these years looked straight into its future. The state's new military-industrial economic foundation, its heightened value to a nation increasingly engaged in the Pacific basin, and its revitalized sunbelt appeal would in short order propel it to the first rank among states. 'We have sniffed our destiny,' proclaimed Governor Earl Warren as the war drew to a close."[18]

Of course, not everyone experienced the California Dream or shared in the prosperity of the postwar years. The state's farm workers, for example, suffered long hours in the fields for little money and had very poor living conditions. Black Californians, not welcomed in the suburbs, were often forced to live in overcrowded urban ghettos. Japanese Americans were among the greatest domestic victims of World War II. They were imprisoned in walled camps, lost their personal property and businesses, and were forced to start over when the war ended.

THE POLITICS OF EXPERIENCE: FROM EARL WARREN TO RONALD REAGAN

The only governor to be elected three times in California history, Earl Warren dominated California politics from 1942 to 1953, the early boom years. While elected as a Republican, Warren's even-handed approach, which appealed to both Republicans and Democrats, resulted in a return to nonpartisanship in California politics. According to James E. Gregg, Professor of Political Science at Chico State University, Warren has been described as "[a man] of absolute integrity. He was a man above party, a candidate without a machine, and a political leader and governor whose first loyalty was to pragmatic programs not party ideology." [19]

The Republican Party dominated California during the 1940s and early 1950s. Republicans took every statewide office except attorney general when Earl Warren became governor in 1942. The same was true in the 1950 election.

Under Warren the state moved ahead with an impressive program of public improvements in highways, freeways, and state and institutional buildings. Helped by uninterrupted prosperity, the state operated with a balanced budget. Warren's appointments were for the most part competent, and the entire executive and administrative branches of government functioned with little hint of corruption or venality. Through repeated advocacy of a compulsory health program, Warren roused enthusiasm among liberals while inviting the wrath of reactionaries and the healthcare establishment, including the American Medical Association.

California underwent remarkable changes and growth during the Warren era. His administration worked hard to meet the challenges of population and economic growth. His dedication and determination to meet the needs of the people of California are best expressed in his own words.

> Happiness is best advanced where there is the greatest spirit of harmony, where opportunity in life is equal, where there is no squalor, where the health of all people is protected, and where the dignity of the human personality is recognized without regard to race or creed. None of these things follow from mere numbers. They must be sought after, planned for, and perfected as built-in segments of our social structure. I would urge every university, college, school, church, business and labor group, indeed every family, to face squarely the fact that we have the problem of providing for the happiness of more people than any state in the Union.

And I would emphasize the fact that the millions to whose happiness we are dedicating ourselves are our children and their children. What better heritage could we leave them?[20]

For years Democratic registrants held a three to two numerical edge over Republicans in California and still lost most of the elections. Democrats would win elsewhere in the country, but the Golden State voted its own mind. Republican candidates dominated California politics for three reasons. One was cross-filing, a system whereby a candidate could run for office without disclosing his political affiliation. Originally a Progressive measure intended to end one-party rule, it had instead given the Republicans a near-permanent lease on the state. Even though there were more Democratic registrants in the state, popular candidates of a Republican persuasion did not have to reveal their true party identification when running for office.

Second was the weakness of the state Democratic Party organization. Unlike the Republicans, with their California Republican Assembly, the Democrats lacked a volunteer organization capable of getting out the vote. Third was Earl Warren himself, whose liberal social reforms, such as compulsory health insurance and higher old-age pensions, stole most of the platform out from under the Democrats.

All of this had changed by the 1958 election, however. Warren was no longer governor because President Eisenhower had appointed him to the U.S. Supreme Court. A revision in the cross-filing laws made it necessary for candidates to identify themselves politically. And the Democrats now presided over a strong organization of dedicated volunteers. The latter was the legacy of Adlai Stevenson, a native Californian, though long-time resident of Illinois.

In 1958, then-Attorney General Edmund G. "Pat" Brown, a proven vote getter, was persuaded by prominent Democrats to run for governor. Labor and the California Democratic Committee (CDC) turned out the vote. Brown defeated U.S. Senator William Knowland with an astonishing million-vote plurality to become only the second Democratic governor in California since the turn of the 20th century. Moreover, the Democrats filled all but one of the major state offices, captured control of both houses of the state legislature, and defeated the right-to-work amendment. The right-to-work amendment was viewed as anti-union inasmuch as it stipulated that no person could be denied, or excluded from, employment due to membership or *nonmembership* in a labor organization. If passed, it would have placed legal limitations on union security agreements. Other states considered similar right-to-work amendments, but only Kansas became a right-to-work state.

Brown won re-election in 1962, when he defeated former Vice President Richard Nixon, who had also lost the 1960 presidential election to John F. Kennedy. During his eight years as governor, Pat Brown managed to rack up a number of remarkable accomplishments—at a time when the state was faced with an unprecedented population boom and a host of growth-related problems.

California faced a serious water problem for many years (and still does). While 70 percent of the people lived in southern California, most of the state's water was found in northern California. Most politicians chose to ignore this problem, primarily because of the intense feelings between the two parts of the state. Confronting considerable opposition, Brown gained approval of state bonds to support the Feather River Project, which channels surplus water from the northern portion of the state to the south through a series of aqueducts and canals.

He gained a reputation as the father of California's impressive system of higher education. He spearheaded a revolutionary Master Plan for Higher Education and saw three new university campuses and six new state colleges added to the state's educational system during his administration.

He developed the state's freeway system while working to control air pollution. He also overhauled the executive branch, a move that defined government authority and reduced the cost of state government. He grouped 360 separate boards, agencies, and commissions, many with overlapping functions and each protecting their own authority, creating fewer than eight state agencies. The head of each of these agencies was a member of the governor's cabinet. This not only defined areas of authority, it was instrumental in reducing the cost of state government.[21]

Brown established California's first fair employment practices commission and fought against unfair housing practices. He increased aid to the elderly, raised unemployment insurance, and created an office of consumer counsel. He revised the parole system and recommended strong anti-narcotics programs.[22]

Brown's many accomplishments weren't uniformly admired. Some members of minority groups felt he had not done enough to help them. Others thought he had attempted too much—spending heavily on social programs, education, and the state's infrastructure. Farmers hated him for ending the Bracero program, which brought cheap labor from Mexico. The farm workers felt he had waited too long to end the program. The radical politics on college campuses sparked by the Free Speech Movement begun at UC Berkeley did not help him either.

A conservative backlash in California was triggered in part by the Watts Riots in the summer of 1965 and the radical politics of the young on college campuses. Racially fueled riots were happening across the country, including in California. The spark that set off the Watts Riots, a neighborhood in Los Angeles' South Central area, was the arrest of a 21-year-old African American. When a crowd of onlookers began to shout at the officer who stopped the young man, a second officer was called to the scene. Word spread that the second officer struck some of the hecklers with his baton. Heightened racial tensions, a summer heat wave, and overcrowding in the neighborhood were the kindling needed to incite the riot as word spread about the officer's behavior. Thirty-four people died, more than 1,000 were wounded, and an estimated $200 million in property damage resulted from the riots. The riots did not help Brown's bid for reelection. He lost the 1966 election to former actor and political newcomer Ronald Reagan. Reagan's election marked a shift in California politics from the left to the right.

THE ERA OF CONSERVATIVE POLITICS:
FROM RONALD REAGAN TO GRAY DAVIS

Reagan, who first achieved prominence on the national political stage when he spoke on behalf of Barry Goldwater's presidential campaign in 1964, ran as a citizen politician who claimed that Brown had lost touch with the people. Reagan was re-elected in 1970.

During his eight years in office, Reagan established a conservative record by restricting the size and cost of state government and erasing the deficit inherited from the Brown administration. He balanced the state budget and reformed the welfare system. Reagan and Pat Brown represented opposite views on the role of government. Brown saw government as a vehicle for social change and public works; Reagan in his own words saw:

> Government [not as the] solution to our problems; government is the problem. From time to time we've been tempted to believe that society has become too complex to be managed by self-rule, that government by an elite group is superior to government for, by, and of the people. But if no one among us is capable of governing himself, then who among us has the capacity to govern someone else? All of us together—in and out of government—must bear the burden. The solutions we seek must be equitable with no one group singled out to pay a higher price.[23]

Reagan's rhetoric proved to be somewhat inconsistent with his public policies. For example, after having run on a platform against high taxes, Reagan increased taxes several times during his administration in order to balance the budget. The one issue he stood firm on, however, was his determination to bring "law and order" back to the troubled campuses of the state university and college system. He fired the liberal president of UC Berkeley, Clark Kerr, and mobilized the National Guard to quell a showdown with student radicals who were determined to convert a parking lot into a "people's park" at Berkeley.

Reagan's greatest legacy was turning the state from the politics of the left to the right. For example, he cut the rate of increase in state spending, tightened but did not eliminate welfare provisions, and vetoed bills to establish bilingual education. One of Reagan's more controversial policies—and one we continue to live with daily on our streets—was the closure of most mental health outpatient clinics and the firing of nearly 3,000 mental hospital employees.

On the flip side, Reagan supported automatic cost-of-living increases in welfare, increased state support to higher education, and decriminalized possession of small amounts of marijuana. He signed a liberalized abortion law, spoke against a state proposition that would have barred homosexual teachers from public schools, and created strong antipollution agencies.

Jerry Brown, the son of Edmund "Pat" Brown, followed Reagan into the governor's mansion in 1974. Actually, Jerry Brown chose not to live in the mansion, preferring instead more humble lodgings befitting his Jesuit Catholic background. Brown came into office shortly after the Watergate scandal hurt the Republican Party throughout the United States, resulting in an upsurge in Democratic registration in California. Although the nation experienced two major recessions during his eight years in office, Brown managed to help create 2.2 million jobs, and he supported a billion-dollar tax cut, moving California from the 4th highest taxed state to the 23rd.

Jerry Brown represented traditional liberal values. He supported civil rights legislation, opposed the death penalty, and favored labor and unions. He also advocated for environmental protection (at the time a relatively new issue on the public agenda). For example, he adopted the strictest air pollution control laws in the country and banned toxic chemicals that were still allowed at the federal level. He halted construction of nuclear power plants in California and put the state in the forefront of conservation and the development and use of alternative energy sources.

Jerry Brown established the California Arts Council, which is made up solely of practicing artists. He repealed criminal penalties for private sexual acts between consenting adults and signed an executive order banning discrimination based on sexual orientation. Brown appointed many women and minorities to important positions in his administration—especially the judiciary. He appointed the first woman as chief justice of the California Supreme Court, Rose Bird.

Brown was not, however, a strong believer in an expanded role of government. Unlike many of his fellow liberals, including his father, Jerry Brown believed very strongly in the philosophy that "small is better"—describing the times as the "era of limits." He spoke out in favor of people resolving problems more on their own, with less reliance on government intervention.

Brown's appeal to higher personal and political consciousness (he was labeled "Governor Moonbeam" by the press) wore thin on the public as the economy faltered and complex social issues confronted the state and the nation. It did not help that he was frequently absent from the state while he twice sought the presidency (1976 and 1980). As Brown ended his second administration, his popularity had dropped significantly.

George Deukmejian became governor in the year that Los Angeles hosted the very successful 1982 Olympics and the Macintosh computer arrived on the scene—arguably the start of the computer revolution. He left office eight years later as California's aerospace industry was collapsing due to military base closures.

Deukmejian is best described as conservative and cautious. He barely won election in 1982 against Tom Bradley, the African American mayor of Los Angeles. A strong opponent of gun control, Deukmejian benefited from the fact that gun-control advocates qualified a handgun-registration initiative for the statewide ballot. The proposition caused large numbers of white, conservative voters to turn out on Election Day both to defeat the gun-control measure and to elect Deukmejian as governor.

Those close to Deukmejian referred to him as the "Iron Duke" for his tough handling of the legislature. He believed strongly in fostering economic growth and deregulation of industry—the opposite view of his predecessor, Jerry Brown. In the 1980s, California's population exploded 25 percent. The Deukmejian administration felt it had to do everything possible to assist the private sector in creating jobs. This stress forced the weakening of environmental laws, including those that covered safe drinking water and toxic enforcement.

As a former attorney general, Deukmejian was a strong "law and order" governor. He built 14 new prisons during his eight years in office. He was a strong advocate for the death penalty and worked to strengthen laws to assist the police and courts in prosecuting criminals. When asked why he ran for the office of governor, he replied, "attorney generals don't appoint judges—governors do." During his two terms in office, Deukmejian appointed more than 1,000 judges. By the time he left office, he had appointed a majority of the state Supreme Court justices—an important legacy for any governor.

Deukmejian was often described as a man out of step with the changing times in California. During the 1980s, California experienced a serious recession, high inflation, shifts in its economic base due, in part, to the ending of the cold war, and dramatic changes in immigration and other demographic patterns. Everything was changing, except government itself. Deukmejian's approach to governing and his public policies were unresponsive to the changed conditions in California.

His successor and fellow Republican, Pete Wilson, faced many challenges when he assumed office in 1991. Wilson came into office at a time when California was experiencing a downturn in its economy and a serious budget deficit. Wilson inherited a $10 billion budget deficit from Deukmejian. The inability of Wilson and the legislature to agree on a budget during his first term resulted in a budget impasse that left the state without a budget for a record 64 days.

Racial conflict impacted Wilson's eight years in office. Demographic studies predicted that around the turn of the 21st century, whites would become a minority. California was becoming more multicultural, with a growing population of Asians, Latinos, and blacks. The Wilson administration and the state led the national movement in 1994 against immigration with the passage of the anti-Latino Proposition 187.

Proposition 187 prohibits public social services to those who cannot establish their status as a U.S. citizen, a lawful permanent resident, or an "alien lawfully admitted for a temporary period of time."[24] It also limits attendance at public schools to U.S. citizens and to aliens lawfully admitted to the United States for permanent residence or otherwise authorized to be here.[25]

Wilson supported the equally controversial 1996 initiative, Proposition 209, to end all state affirmative action programs. His strong positions on law and order led him to support the "three strikes and you're out" legislation that sentenced even small-time offenders to life in prison if convicted of a felony for a third time.

In his bid for reelection in 1994, Wilson ran against Jerry Brown's sister, Secretary of State Kathleen Brown. Wilson managed to win even though his popularity was lagging due to the many serious economic and social problems plaguing the state in the 1990s. California's economy had deteriorated, race relations were tense, and the budget stalemate was the longest in state history. Wilson won mainly because Kathleen Brown waged an ineffective campaign, and the public opinion polls showed that many voters felt it wiser to stay the course, rather than change directions during these precarious times.

By the end of Wilson's second term in office, the state had rebounded from its worst economy since the Great Depression. Wilson worked to create a much friendlier climate for business—including tax relief to attract and retain businesses in California and the continuation of Deukmejian's business-friendly environmental regulations—and to improve the state's educational system. His historic education reforms defined California's "education renaissance."

Gray Davis, who defeated Dan Lungren in 1998, was the first Democrat to be elected governor since Jerry Brown, nearly three decades before, and only the third Democrat to hold the office in the 20th century. He was also the first white male since Brown to be nominated by the Democrats. (An African American man and two women were nominated in the interim years.) Davis was the underdog candidate, thought to be too boring and uninspiring to win the election. His strengths were his ability to successfully reach out to the political center and raise millions of dollars—not unlike his contemporary, Bill Clinton.

Davis campaigned on education, healthcare reform, crime prevention, and greater controls on assault weapons. He moved quickly on all of his major campaign promises. His pet education-reform package, which included peer review for teachers, stronger reading programs, and a mandatory high school exit exam, was quickly approved. He successfully pushed for the nation's toughest bans on assault weapons and "Saturday-night specials." Soon after taking office, Davis signed a revolutionary and bipartisan healthcare reform package that, among other things, expands coverage to include breast cancer and mental illnesses like schizophrenia and bipolar disorder, creates a panel to review denial of coverage, and gives patients the right to sue HMOs that place a higher premium on making a profit over the health of their patients.

Davis can be described as walking the middle of the political road. He is pro-choice and pro-death penalty. His policies and politics indicate that he is concerned about the environment, yet he wants to create a pro-business climate in the state. Davis probably described himself best when he said in his State of the State address, "I don't really care which side of the aisle a good idea comes from as long as it will work."

A FINAL WORD

Today, California has an economy that produces $1.2 trillion GSP (Gross State Product) and is the largest state economy in the United States. In fact, California is the fifth-largest producer of goods and services in the world (the rest all being sovereign countries). California's economy grew at a healthy pace during much of the 1990s. Starting in 2000, economic growth slowed consider-

A Closer Look

Go to the 1999 California Statistical Abstract (http://www.dof.ca.gov/HTML/FSDATA/stat-abs/toc.htm) and determine the median household income and percentage of population living below the poverty line in your county. What does this say about the income gap in your community?

ably, and with the energy crisis (see Chapter 2) and collapse of the dot-com sector of the economy, the fear is that it will continue to falter for several years. The terrorist attacks on September 11, 2001, hurt the economy. Tourism is down, and homeland security measures are costing the state millions of dollars. Governor Davis and the legislature struggle to close a $35 billion budget deficit for fiscal year 2003-2004.

The economy shifted to new bases of employment and industry in the 1990s. The California economy no longer is heavily reliant on aerospace and defense-related manufacturing. During the 1990s, California emerged with strengths in advanced telecommunications, multimedia, biotechnology, Internet services and equipment, entertainment, tourism, business services, construction, biotechnology, wine making, foreign trade, professional services, and high-tech manufacturing. Although many of these industries were hit at the turn of the century, and post–September 11, it is expected that they will fuel economic recovery and growth in the state.

Many California families were relatively worse off than before the boom times of the 1990s. Not everyone benefited from the dot-com mania. The 2001–2002 recession did not help matters. In 2002, the state led the nation in unemployment. There was little across the board wage growth, and a disproportionate number of its citizens lived below the poverty line. Moreover, the purchasing power of most families was lower then than it was two decades before. Families had to work harder and longer just to get by. Not surprisingly, incomes were different according to region—higher in the metropolitan and coastal areas and lower in the rural and interior valley areas—and by other characteristics like race and ethnicity.[26] The unemployment rate remains high in 2003, with nearly 7 percent unemployment in Northern California.

The gap between California's rich and poor is the sixth widest in the nation, and the gap between wealthy and middle-income families with children is the third widest in the nation. According to Jean Ross, executive director of the California Budget Project, "The rising tide of the recent recovery has not lifted all boats. The purchasing power of three out of five California families with children has dropped since the mid-1970s, and the incomes of four out of five families declined since the mid-1980s after adjusting for inflation." Ross goes on to say, "Most Californians have received only minimal benefits from the current recovery [1995–1998]. Wages and incomes are below where they were in 1989 and inequity is on the rise. While recent wage gains are a welcome

---

A Closer Look

How would you describe the community you are from? What are the demographic, social and economic issues, and voting patterns in your community?

---

reversal of longer-term trends, most of California's working families are still playing catch-up. [Furthermore] these recent gains will be difficult to sustain as economic growth slows." [27]

Box 1.1, found at the beginning of this chapter, identified many of the social, economic, and environmental issues that confront this great state. True, it continues to be a land of prosperity, but not for everyone. In the next chapter, we discuss many of the issues that form California's public agenda. They include energy, education, land and water use, economic opportunity for everyone, population growth, the environment, and crime prevention.

As democratic citizens, we have an obligation to be informed about these issues and to make known to California's leaders our views. The value of citizen participation in California politics was embodied in the Bear Flag movement of 1845. William B. Ide summed up the political credo of the Bear Flaggers when he said, "that a Government to be prosperous and happifying in its tendency must originate with its people . . . that its Citizens are its Guardians, its officers are in its Servants, and its Glory their reward." [28] We have an obligation to help determine what kind of place California will be for ourselves and for generations to follow.

ADDITIONAL RESOURCES

Ambrose, Stephen. 2000. *Nothing Like It in the World: The Men Who Built the Transcontinental Railroad 1863–1869.* New York: Simon and Schuster.

California Department of Finance. 2000. California Statistical Abstract. Available at http://www.dof.ca.gov/HTML/FS_DATA/stat-abs/toc.htm.

Hundley, Norris, Jr. 2001. *The Great Thirst: Californians and Water:*

A History, Revised Edition. Berkeley: University of California Press.

Rawls, James J., and Walton Bean. 1998. *California: An Interpretive History* (7th Edition). Boston: McGraw-Hill.

Schrag, Peter. 1998. *Paradise Lost: California's Experience, America's Future.* Berkeley: University of California Press.

NOTES

1. Oakland Museum of California, *Gold Fever: California's Gold Rush* (New York: W.W. Norton & Company, Inc., 2000), 3.

2. Philip L. Fradkin, *The Seven States of California: A Human and Natural History* (New York: Holt & Co., 1995), 3.

3. John W. Caughey, *California,* 2nd edition (Englewood Cliffs, NJ: Prentice-Hall, Inc., 1953), 30–45.

4. Fradkin, *The Seven States of California: A Human and Natural History,* 5.

5. Pat Ooley, "An Overview of the History of Constitutional Provisions Dealing with State Governance," September 13, 2000, l. http://www.library.ca.gov/CCRC/reports/html/hs-state-governance.html.

6. Ibid., 1.

7. Arthur Mann, ed., *The Progressive Era: Liberal Renaissance or Liberal Failure?* (New York: Holt, Rinehart and Winston, 1963), 2.

8. See Kevin Starr, *Inventing the Dream: California through the Progressive Era* (New York: Oxford University Press, 1985), 199–200.

9. Royce D. Delmatier, Clarence F. McIntosh, Earl G. Waters, eds., *The Rumble of California Politics 1848–1970* (New York: John Wiley & Sons, 1970), 122.

10. Jeffrey I. Chapman, "California: The Enduring Crisis," in Steven D. Gold, ed., *The Fiscal Crisis of the States: Lessons for the Future* (Washington, DC: Georgetown University Press, 1995), 105.

11. Alan Brinkley, *The Unfinished Nation: A Concise History of the American People,* 3rd ed. (Boston, MA: McGraw Hill, 2000), 629.

12. Ibid., 628–630.

13. James N. Gregory, *American Exodus* (New York: Oxford University Press, 1980), 23.

14. Ibid., 23.

15. Ibid., 25.

16. The Bracero program takes its name from a Spanish term meaning "strong-armed ones." Through the Bracero program many thousands of Mexicans were brought to California to work on the state's farms. This program provided cheap labor to farmers, a powerful lobbying group in Sacramento. Unfortunately, the farm laborers were treated poorly, living in substandard housing and given little or no health care.

17. Thomas Muller, *The Fourth Wave: California's Newest Immigrants, A Summary* (Washington, DC: The Urban Institute Press, 1964).

18. Gregory, *American Exodus.* 173.

19. Delmatier et al., *The Rumble of California Politics: 1848–1970,* 301.

20. Ibid., 325–326.

21. Gary G. Hamilton and Nicole Woolsey Biggart, *Governor Reagan, Governor Brown: A Sociology of Executive Power,* (New York: Columbia University Press, 1984), 62–64.

22. Delmatier et al., *The Rumble of California Politics: 1848–1970,* 341–357.

23. Paul D. Erickson, *Reagan Speaks* (New York: New York University Press, 1985), 143.

24. Stanley Mailman, "California's Proposition 187 and Its Lessons," *New York Law Journal* (3), January 3, 1995. http://www.ssbb.com/article1.html.

25. Ibid.

26. Jean Ross, California Budget Project.

27. Ibid.

28. Caughey, *California,* 232.

2

California at the New Millennium: The Public Policy Challenges

Public policy issues are not simply obscure issues over which policy "wonks" argue and disagree—they affect real people and create important changes in our lives. The energy crisis faced by California today is an important example of how public policy issues emerge suddenly and quickly and then, just as suddenly, can disappear. Energy rapidly became the most important issue in the state for many citizens during 2000 and 2001—and became the defining issue of Governor Gray Davis's first term as governor. During that time, the crisis dominated the media, showing up almost daily on the front page of many state newspapers.

Every aspect of the public policy process and every player were involved: the governor worked to license additional power plants and keep prices low; the state legislature met in special session and created new legislation to alleviate the crisis; and state workers, the bureaucracy, participated by purchasing electricity, monitoring electricity usage and need, and by implementing blackouts. Throughout, there were allegations that there was adequate energy available and that the utility companies created the crisis, that government advisors owned stock in the utility companies, and that the utility companies were making money off of the crisis. There is now evidence to support many of those allegations, which are under investigation by federal regulators.

Some of the results of this public policy crisis? Individual consumers paid more out of their pocket for electricity and natural gas and suffered the inconvenience of rolling blackouts, state businesses suffered declines in productivity from the black-outs and increased energy costs themselves, the state budget reserve at that time was substantially diminished as the state bought power, and the state economy as a whole suffered, which had repercussions for the national economy as well.

Public policy, no matter the source, does affect all of us.

Many challenges, dilemmas, and opportunities face California in the new millennium. Decisions made now about issues such as the energy crisis, education, crime, health care, and the economy will determine the fate of the state for some time to come. As a possible indication of the complexity and rapid change facing all Californians, the policy issues that the public sees as the most important facing the state change rapidly (see Table 2.1). In April 1998, California voters believed the most important issue was crime, followed closely by education. Only one year later (September 1999), the concerns about crime were supplanted by greater concerns for schools and education. By 2001, the energy crisis, as symbolized by high electricity prices and electricity deregulation, had taken center stage in the public's eyes. Just one year later (2002), the energy crisis had diminished in importance and schools and the economy had once again taken the forefront in the minds of California voters.

ENERGY CRISIS

While many Californians had the impression that the energy crisis was a new event for the state, the crisis of 2000–2001 was one that has been building for some time and was a product of many complex events. California's energy crisis had its roots in policy, regulatory, and utility decisions made years ago as well as in California's increasing population growth and demand for electricity. Table 2.2 and Table 2.3 provide a chronology of events in the crisis and a guide to the many acronyms for the agencies and companies that play important roles in the energy arena.

The crisis can be immediately traced back to 1996, when the state deregulated the electricity industry in the Electric Utility Restructuring Act of 1996. In the move to electricity deregulation (removing government regulation of electricity markets), this act made energy generation a competitive process, allowing electricity generators to compete with one another to buy electricity at the lowest price possible from whatever supplier they liked. The intention at the time was to use the marketplace to reduce the price of electricity for both

Table 2.1 California Voter Views on the Most Important Public Policy Issue Facing California, April 1998, September 1999, July 2001, and October 2002

Most Important Policy Issue in April 1998	Most Important Policy Issue in September 1999	Most Important Policy Issue in July 2001	Most Important Policy Issue in October 2002 *
Crime (Selected by 28%)	Schools, education (selected by 31%)	Electricity prices, deregulation (selected by 56%)	Schools, education (21%)
Education (20%)	Crime, gangs (8%)	Schools, education (9%)	Jobs and the economy (14%)
Immigration (7%)	Immigration (7%)	Jobs, the economy, unemployment (5%)	State budget (7%)
Economy (5%)	Guns, gun control (5%)	Growth, population, overpopulation (4%)	Taxes (7%)
Drugs (4%)	Jobs, the economy (3%)	Immigration, illegal immigration (4%)	Electricity cost and supply/ energy (6%)
Growth (4%)	Poverty, welfare, the homeless, the poor (3%)	Crime, gangs (3%)	Health care (4%)
Poverty (4%)	Health care, HMO reform (3%)	Environment, pollution (2%)	Environment (3%)
State government (3%)	Environment, pollution (3%)	Housing costs, housing availability (2%)	Campaign money/ethics (3%)
Taxes (2%)	Taxes (2%)	Poverty, the poor, the homeless, welfare (2%)	Immigration (2%)
Values (2%)	Race relations, ethnic tensions (2%)	Drugs (1%)	Crime and gangs (2%)

SOURCES: Mark Baldassare and the Public Policy Institute of California. 2002, 2001, 1999, 1998. *PPIC Statewide Survey: Californians and Their Government.* San Francisco: Public Policy Institute of California, October 2002; July 2001; September, 1999; April 1998.

*The question was, "Which one issue would you like to hear the gubernatorial candidates talk about before the November 5 election?"

generators and consumers. The act also allowed consumers to choose their own electricity generation supplier, created the Cal PX (California Power Exchange—where electricity would be bought and sold), and created the Independent System Operator (ISO). The ISO was to manage the state's transmission facilities and give all utilities an equal opportunity to use them for transferring their electricity—rather than have each utility own its own.

Table 2.2 Time Line of the 2000–2001 California Energy Crisis

Date	Event
1996	The Electric Utility Restructuring Act, which makes energy generation in California a competitive process (deregulates it), becomes law
Summer 2000	Electricity prices in San Diego rise precipitously
June 14	100,000 San Francisco Bay Area residents experience rolling blackouts
July 27	Governor Davis asks federal regulators (Federal Energy Regulatory Commission) to extend the caps on the prices of wholesale electricity
August 30/ September 6	The California legislature adopts electricity rate caps for San Diego residents (AB 265); governor signs the bill
November 1	FERC declines to put cap on wholesale electricity prices, recommends long-term contracts for utilities with electricity generators to stabilize prices
November 29	In frustration, consumers file a $1 billion class action lawsuit accusing 14 energy companies of manipulating prices
December 7	ISO issues Stage 3 alert (the most serious) and warns of rolling blackouts
December 13	Federal energy secretary orders 12 generating companies to sell power to PG&E and Southern California Edison to prevent more serious outages
December 16	Governor Davis calls special session of the legislature and reserves $1 billion in the 2001–2002 budget to deal with power crisis
January 3, 2001	Legislature convenes special session to deal with crisis
January 4	The PUC allows PG&E and Southern CA Edison (SCE) to raise rates
January 17	Rolling blackouts are ordered across California for the first time; Governor Davis declares a state of emergency
February 1	Legislature authorizes the state to buy power with long-term contracts
February 2	Governor Davis signs the bill, which also authorizes the state to sell up to $10 billion of bonds to buy electricity
March 27	PUC approves a rate increase to support the struggling PGE and SCE
April 5	Governor Davis releases a full plan to resolve the state's energy problems—aimed at increasing power supply, improving conservation, and stabilizing the electricity industry
April 6	PG&E filed for reorganization under Chapter 11 in U.S. Bankruptcy Court due to unreimbursed energy costs of up to $300 million per month
April 9	Governor Davis announces an agreement with Southern California Edison to purchase their transmission system so that SCE may recover financially
April 25	The FERC announces a plan to stabilize the California energy market
May 15	PUC passes rate increases with incentives for conservation
May	Governor Davis signs other bills passed by legislature to create the California Consumer Power and Conservation Financing Authority and speed up applications for new power plants

SOURCES: Partially based upon: "Davis Neglected Key Strategy in Power Crisis" and "Road to the Energy Crisis," *San Francisco Chronicle,* February 4, 2001, A1, A18; "California Electric Energy Crisis," U.S. Department of Energy. Available at http://www.eia.doe.gov/cneaf/ electricity/california/subsequentevents.html; Chronology of the California Energy Crisis, Pacific Gas & Electric, available at http://biz.yahoo.com/rf/010208/n08388011.html.

Table 2.3 Players in the California Energy Crisis

Acronym	Title of Agency	Role/Significance
Cal PX	California Power Exchange	The electricity market created by the 1996 electricity deregulation act—electricity is bought and sold here
DOE	U.S. Department of Energy	The U.S. Department of Energy has regulatory responsibilities in power generation and sale; has used these to require out-of-state regulators to sell power in California
EOB	Electricity Oversight Board	Created by the 1996 deregulation legislation, it oversees the electricity market and the Independent System Operator; the board is also responsible for representing the state before the FERC
FERC	Federal Energy Regulatory Commission	Regulates wholesale prices and other aspects of energy throughout the United States
ISO	Independent System Operator	Agency that monitors electricity and natural gas supplies and declares blackouts and operates most of the state's utility grid
PGE	Pacific Gas and Electric	Investor-owned state electricity supplier who declared bankruptcy in 2001, during the crisis
PUC or CPUC	California Public Utilities Commission	Regulates the retail prices of electricity, determines the level of profit that utility companies might make, and regulates other activities of utility companies
SCE	Southern California Edison	One of the major investor-owned electric utility companies

In addition to electricity deregulation, the crisis grew from several other factors:

- At the time of the 1996 act, the price of electricity in California was 9.48 cents per kilowatt hour (the tenth highest in the country) but would soon start growing.

- Demand for electricity among California consumers was increasing steadily (11.3 percent from 1990 to 1999)—something that would serve to increase prices further.

- In-state electric generating capacity declined by 1.7 percent during 1990 to 1999, further reducing the supply.

- No new plants had been built to accommodate the new population in the state in more than a decade.

- More of the state's needed power was to come from out-of-state (up to 7 to 11 gigawatts), a very precarious position for California consumers.

- Reduced rainfall in the Northwest reduced water levels and subsequently reduced hydroelectric power generation.

- In early 2000, many of the electrical plants and generating capacity were off-line for repairs, further reducing available power by 10 gigawatts.

- The high-voltage electrical lines that move electricity between Northern and Southern California became overloaded and reduced the ability to transfer power back and forth.[1]

Despite these emerging factors, the new deregulated system worked moderately well as long as electricity prices remained low. However, many of these factors began to converge, and in the summer of 2000, prices began increasing throughout the state, particularly in San Diego. Consumers in the San Francisco Bay Area then began to experience rolling blackouts, the loss of electricity in selected communities that then got their electricity back while others lost theirs, due to a shortage of generating capacity.

Rolling blackouts across the state continued in December and throughout spring 2001, although the much-anticipated summer of rolling blackouts did not actually occur. At that point, the three investor-owned utilities in California—Pacific Gas & Electric (PG&E), Southern California Edison (SCE), and San Diego Gas & Electric (SDG&E)—began to face severe financial difficulties. This difficulty was due to many factors but was exacerbated by having to pay much higher utility costs while being limited by the Public Utility Commission from passing on the higher rates to consumers. With independent power generators reluctant to sell power to them because of these difficulties, the situation deteriorated further.[2] By April 6, PG&E had filed for Chapter 11 bankruptcy. Allegations that both PG&E and SCE had paid high bonuses to their executives did little to dissuade the public, who questioned whether or not the crisis was real, and helped to enhance the already widespread distrust of the utility companies.

Under Governor Gray Davis, the legislature was called into special session in January 2001 to deal with the crisis and public policy and regulatory initiatives began to emerge. Together, they authorized the state to engage in long-term contracts and buy power itself for sale to consumers; later, up to $10 billion in bonds were authorized to pay for these electricity sales. The Public Utility Commission allowed PG&E and SCE to raise their rates, although requirements for conservation incentives and assistance to low-income individuals were included in these measures.

The state also responded with new fast-track procedures for approving new power plants to add to the state's generating capacity. Under these new rules, three plants capable of generating over 300 megawatts were operational by mid-July, another plant was schedule to be completed by September 1, another three were coming on-line by June 2002, and another nine were scheduled to be finished by June 2004. Many other plants are in the planning and review stages.[3]

A Closer Look

Go to the Staff Fact-Finding Investigation of Western Markets (http://www.ferc.fed.us/ electric/bulkpower/ pa02-2/pa02-2.htm) to find the status of the continuing investigation into whether the California energy crisis was real or the result of a conspiracy among energy companies.

Go to the Web site of the California Independent System Operator to see the current status of electricity supply, forecasted demand, and actual demand (http://www.caiso.com/ SystemStatus.html). Ideally, the supply should be greater than forecasted and actual demand. If forecasted demand is greater than actual demand, this could mean that consumers and businesses are saving or that the weather is cooler than anticipated. What is the current status of the state's electricity supply?

New electricity prices were approved although with conservation incentives included. These incentives were successful, as electricity usage declined in some months by more than 11 to 12 percent, compared with the previous year.

The shocking result of these circumstances is that evidence eventually emerged to support the supposition of many during the crisis that it was manufactured, seemingly coming out of nowhere to explode as a critical issue. To many, even the many factors cited above did not add up to create a crisis of the size that emerged. The Federal Energy Regulatory Commission is currently investigating allegations that energy companies like the now-discredited and bankrupt Enron were in reality part of a widespread conspiracy to defraud California consumers and make money off of the engineered crisis.[4] If these allegations are proven to be true, then it is possible that California can retrieve some of the many resources that were spent on the crisis—but the political capital and consumer trust that was expended is irretrievable.

In the short term, many of these measures had some impact. However, the long-term impact of the crisis was felt in many different ways. In order to pay for electricity, the multibillion-dollar budget surplus held by the state of California at the beginning of the crisis declined by two-thirds from its status in 1999–2000[5] and ended with a budget deficit of $21 billion for 2003–2004. Energy conservation grew in importance and remained a constant. Environmental concerns, brought about by the fast tracking of numerous new electricity power generation plants, have increased. No policy actions are without consequences—and this is very obvious from examining the state's energy crisis. The level of resources dedicated to solving the energy crisis kept those resources from being available for solving other issues. In spring 2003, legislation was being discussed to end the state's experiment with electricity deregulation, which is now widely considered a failure, but to date, this has not occurred.

EDUCATION: THE GOVERNOR'S
INITIAL TOP PRIORITY

Given the world economy in which California now operates, education promises to be even more important than in the past. How else will students participate, contribute, and compete in this global economy except with an education well-grounded in writing, communication, mathematical and technical skills, and an understanding of their historical and cultural roots? With an economy moving away from traditional manufacturing to one based increasingly upon a knowledge-based economy, proficiency in these areas will become even more important.

The growing levels of poverty in society[6] is one reason Gray Davis, the first Democratic California governor in 16 years, had started his term with education as his number one priority (at least until California's energy crisis exploded). In his first State of the State speech, Governor Davis said, "My first priority—in fact my first, second and third priority—is education. And my goal is to set higher expectations for everyone involved in our schools: students and parents, teachers and administrators. This, I believe, is our duty to the future."[7]

The most important challenges facing education in California today are funding, quality and access. Having adequate funds to pay for quality education is always a challenge; determining how to build a quality educational system while making sure that everyone has access to the same levels of quality are equally difficult challenges.

Funding of K–12 education has been a significant issue in California for some years. By 1995–1996, California had fallen to fifteenth from the bottom among states in per-pupil funding of K–12 public education ($5,108), while the national average was $6,146.[8] By 2000–2001, California's per-pupil expenditure was $6,387, which was the thirty-third highest in the nation, seven places higher than two years previously.[9]

In 1988 and 1990, California voters passed two initiatives in an attempt to improve these dismal statistics. Proposition 98 and Proposition 111 guaranteed a minimum amount of funding of 40 percent for K–14 (including community college education) each year.

Related to school funding is the issue of the quality of the education paid for by voters. According to the U.S. Department of Education, the average student achievement in mathematics in California ranked below that of the nation as a whole in 1990, 1992, and in 1996. In 2000, 52 percent of eighth graders showed at least basic proficiency in mathematics.[10] Although improved, these test results still have created a great deal of concern about the effectiveness of education in the state of California.[11] Access to equal education levels of education is also an issue—in California as well as elsewhere around the country.

In an effort to provide accountability for California's public education, Governor Davis's Department of Education developed an incentive program,

---

A Closer Look

Go to the Web site for the California Secretary of Education and the Academic Performance Index Program (http://www.ose.ca.gov/saa/index .html) and find the Academic Performance Index (API) scores for the schools nearest you. Are they what you expected to find? Why or why not?

---

adopted in April 1999, for K–12 schools based upon school performance, judged by a scoring system called the Academic Performance Index (API). The API sets goals for all schools; those schools that meet their goals receive financial awards.

After schools implement their plans and work for a year, schools that do not then improve face a series of sanctions, including reassignment of personnel or even school closing.[12] Those schools that did improve shared a fund of $150 million. These plans were first implemented in spring 2000 with the release of the first API scores by the state. Although plagued by technical difficulties with the scoring, the scores continue to be used to judge the performance of K–12 schools and their ability to educate their students.

The governor's education policy focuses special attention on reading skills for children up to third grade. The policy adds responsibilities for all players in the educational system. "No one gets a free ride," Davis said. "Students will be tested. Teachers will be reviewed. Principals will be held to account and parents will be urged to take greater responsibility."

In the 2000–2001 budget presented for approval to the California legislature, Governor Davis proposed additional new incentives and aid for teachers and potential teachers in order to continue to enhance the educational system. In order to improve the quality of the state education provided to students, the major initiatives fell among several categories, including direct funds to schools to increase per-pupil expenditures, funds to the state universities for teacher training, and incentives to schools who improved their API scores. Among the initiatives finally approved by the legislature and then signed into law by the governor were:

- A 7.5 percent increase in per pupil spending for K–12 education (to $6,801);
- Tax credits for teachers
- Funds to increase the salaries of beginning teachers
- Funds to pay for professional development seminars for teachers
- Funds to improve access to computers and technology for students and teachers
- Bonuses for those schools that met or exceeded their API goals[13]

Table 2.4 Projected Enrollments in California Institutions of Higher Education, Fall 2010

	Community Colleges	California State University Campuses	University of California Campuses
Fall 1999 Enrollments	1,475,000	349,804	173,570
Fall 2010 Enrollments	2,003,918	479,485	229,724
Number of Additional Students	528,918	129,681	56,154
Percent Change	35.86%	37.07%	32.35%

SOURCE: Based on California Postsecondary Education Commission data, http://www.cpec.ca.gov/PressRelease/EnrTables.htm.

However, the looming budget deficit in 2002–2003 will impact education as well as other state services. Many counties are already shedding their lowered class sizes and some districts are planning to. Another initiative discussed by the legislature, to eliminate state income taxes for teachers, was not approved. Whether these initiatives can continue, given the state's looming budget deficit, remains to be seen.

The concerns seen in K–12 education are mirrored in the institutions for higher learning. Community colleges and the two- and four-year public education institutions in California—the California State University and the University of California systems—are expecting enormous changes in their student base over the next 15 to 20 years as demographic trends in the state change. These demographic changes will have an impact on the funding, quality, and access of higher education.

There are some significant trends in the age distribution of California's potential students. The baby boom generation is moving into their 50s, away from the education system but still in the prime of their working lives. Their children are currently the prime age for higher education. Finally, a new baby boom generation is being created as record birth rates are expanding the 0 to 17 age population. The sheer numbers of these young people will produce additional stresses on the educational system in California.

According to the California Postsecondary Education Commission (CPEC), an estimated 455,000 new students will be seeking access to California's public colleges or universities between 1993 and 2005.[14] Table 2.4 presents these projections.

The community college system and both the University of California and the California State University systems are preparing for the arrival of these students, known as "Tidal Wave II," and the serious questions they create about the state's ability and willingness to pay for an extended system of postsecondary education. While the increasing demand is clear, the ability to pay for it is not. The operating expenses of California institutions of higher education have grown faster than the inflation rate for the past 30 years. At the same time, state legislative financing has not kept pace, nor have student tuition increases made up the difference. The result is increasing financial strain on the higher education system, much as is seen at the K–12 level.[15] Further, the large cohort of faculty who were hired to teach in those institutions during the 1960s are retiring in large numbers, leaving a potential gap between the number of students and the number of faculty who are needed to teach them.

The higher education system is also undergoing what appear to be significant changes from the educational system suggested by the California Master Plan of the 1960s. This Master Plan provided a guarantee that higher education would be available to all those in California who wished to participate, through three differentiated segments of higher education—the community college system, the University of California, and the California State University system. Partly due to "Tidal Wave II," the ability to provide access to all those who demand it in the three systems is seriously in doubt as many institutions in both systems are "impacted" and not able to admit all those who are supposed to be admitted, according to the California Master Plan.

Today, however, it appears that the Tidal Wave came in Southern California but not as quickly in Northern California. Enrollments at CSU campuses during the 2000–2001 Academic Year have been quite skewed towards the southern part of the state. By fall 2001, 18 of the 22 CSU campuses, mostly in southern California, showed enrollment increases, but four, mostly in northern California, showed no increase or declines; but by fall 2003 most of the northern campuses were also seeing increases.[16]

THE ENVIRONMENT: BALANCING
GROWTH AND PRESERVATION

As an indicator of the depth of the importance of environmental issues, a June 2002 survey of Californians found that 70 percent believed that California's environmental problems were a threat to them personally. For the respondents to the survey, the top issues were:

- Air pollution (34 percent)
- Growth, development, and sprawl (13 percent)
- Water, ocean, and beach pollution (12 percent)
- Water supply (9 percent)
- Traffic congestion (5 percent)
- Pollution in general (5 percent)[17]

Why these results? Pollution is on the rise as a result of the millions of cars and thousands of factories in the state. California's natural resources, especially its water supply, are under strain because of population growth. The demand for water is increasingly outstripping California's natural reserves. The lack of water is bound to have severe economic, ecological, and demographic consequences for the state. These consequences include water restrictions, more strict curbs on growth and development, and increased droughts. And California has more endangered species than any other state: 283 at the last count.

What is clear is that the very amenities and necessities that brought so many to California (clear air and water, open space, beautiful landscapes, low crime rate, and jobs) now seem in danger. With the state as a leader in the environmental movement since the publication of Rachael Carson's *Silent Spring*,[18] California's laws, which are designed to protect air and water quality and to reduce toxic and solid waste, are among the strictest in the nation. From the founding of the Sierra Club in 1892 to the antipollution initiatives of the 1970s, California has led the country in encouraging environmental protection and serving as a model to the rest of the country. Today, California can serve as an example of what can go wrong in the environment as a result of uncontrolled growth.

Urban Sprawl and Growth

Fully two-thirds of California's citizens live in the coastal zones of the state— particularly around the San Francisco Bay Area and Los Angeles basin.[19] These areas are experiencing some of the greatest growth, with a 14.3 and 16.2 percent increase from 1989 to 1999. The growth is increasing the development and water demand pressures on California's coastal zones, also some of the most vulnerable areas in the state.

Urban and suburban sprawl, low-density development patterns that take up more land than compact and high-density development, also increase the pressures upon other areas within the state. As a result of the lower numbers of houses or offices built upon tracts of land under this pattern, traffic increases, green spaces shrink, and residents and businesses require more land. As the demand for land grows, prices rise, and competition for undeveloped land increases. This pattern places renewed pressure upon California farmers to sell and convert their land into more suburban or urban uses. The loss of productive farmland reduces the state's ability to feed its growing population.

Every state has lost prime farmland to urban development, but California ranks tenth among states with the greatest loss of high-quality farmland— mainly in the Sacramento and San Joaquin Valleys of Central California, the Central Coastal area of the state, and the Imperial Valley.[20]

Water Resources and Water Policy

Since California is currently home to one in eight Americans, includes four of the country's largest cities, and expects additional population growth in the future, adequate safe and clean water is essential to all residents and for all uses (agricultural, urban, and recreation). The California Department of Water Resources estimates that there are water shortages of 1.6 million acre feet (MAF)

A Closer Look

Using resources like the California Environmental Protection Agency (http://www.calepa.ca.gov), the California Resources Agency (http://ceres.ca.gov/cra), and the federal Environmental Protection Agency (http://www.epa.gov) and local resources, develop an environmental profile for your own community. How would you describe the pollution and environment in your area?

---

in years in which the state is without a drought. In drought years, the shortage is much greater—5.1 MAF.[21] With a projected population growth to 59 million by the year 2050[22] and the memory of the 1987–1992 drought and the 1997 flood in Northern and Central California still fresh in many minds, the availability of sufficient water in the right time and place will become even more critical.

The seriousness of water and water policy to the state of California is illustrated by the fact that on March 7, 2000, California voters approved the Safe Drinking Water, Clean Water, Watershed Protection and Flood Protection Act—a $1.97 billion bond issue—a major proposition and piece of public policy. This act promised to move California toward cleaner and safer water through instituting more effective flood control measures. It also promised to improve the water supply infrastructure, protect crucial state watershed areas, enhance flood protection programs, and improve water cleanliness and water conservation efforts.

Future efforts at supporting the water supply and managing California's "most precious natural resource" are under way. The Department of Water Resources plan, "California's Water Future: A Framework for Action," lays out options and strategies for dealing with the hard choices ahead for the state. Many groups with conflicting interests spent hours preparing this plan and developing compromises that would hopefully allow for multiple uses of the water supply. Farmers, environmentalists, city officials, fishery interests, and state government all have their own, different ideas of how to ensure that their own water needs are met in the future.

Some of the most important conflicts concern where the water should go. Should it be diverted to urban areas to provide for residents there, or to farmers, or to rivers to provide adequate supplies for fish? Underneath these crucial conflicts lie the necessity of having clean water for all of these purposes and the fact that some of these uses contribute to the pollution levels of the water supply.

One December 1999 step taken to increase the safety of the water supply was banning the gasoline additive MTBE (methyl tertiary butyl ether), beginning in 2002. Initially thought to result in reduced air pollution from automobile emissions, recent findings have suggested this reduction was not actually occurring. In addition, the fact that there is evidence that MTBE leaches into and contaminates the water supply led to the recent action.[23]

Toxic Wastes and Pollution

Air quality has also been a concern for California. Over the past 30 years, federal, state, and local agencies have implemented many programs to improve air quality, both emissions and concentrations of specific pollutants, in California. Air quality improvement programs have increased automobile emission standards, established cleaner fuels, and created other tougher standards for emissions. The results from these programs have been at least partially successful.

Acid rain is a dangerous pollutant produced by sulfur dioxide (SO_2) and nitrogen oxides (NO_X) being emitted into the air from utilities, industrial plants, transportation, and combustion processes. In 1980, California contributed 70,078 tons of sulfur dioxide into the air. By the third quarter of 2002, the amount of sulfur dioxide had been reduced to 168.9 tons.[24] An enormous reduction in the components of acid rain had been achieved over the past 20 years.

However, while improvements in air quality from reductions in acid rain have been made, ozone (O_3, a gas that, when it is present in the atmosphere, shields the Earth from harmful ultraviolet radiation), particulates, and carbon monoxide still pose air quality problems. California contains three of the top ten urban areas with ozone levels exceeding nationally established minima. Riverside–San Bernardino ranked the highest for ozone levels during the 1995 to 1997 period while the Los Angeles area ranked third. These statistics reflect an improvement since only ten years ago California would have had the top four spots on the national ranking.[25] Particulate matter remains a significant problem, with California having the top four of the top six ranked areas in the country.

Coastal Protection

Another important challenge for California is to protect its unique coastline, a roughly 800-mile stretch along the Pacific Ocean. Offshore oil development began off California's coast in the 1860s, but after a highly publicized ten-day well blowout off the coast of Santa Barbara released 80,000 barrels of oil in 1969, action was taken by citizens to protect their coast. Proposition 20, passed in 1972, created the California Coastal Commission and the beginnings of coastal protection planning.

CRIME AND THE JUSTICE SYSTEM

Perceptions of many citizens aside, crime in California as a whole has been steadily declining since 1980 after steadily increasing from 1952 to 1980. At its peak in 1980, there were practically 4,000 crimes per 100,000 population[26] while in 1999, there were just 1,753.3 crimes per 100,000 population. Of these,

Table 2.5 Profile of California Inmates in Prisons, April to June 2002

Characteristic	Numbers/Percentages
Number of Prisoners	75,604
Percent Male	87.5
Percent Committed Felonies	71.9
Percent Inmates in Maximum-Security Housing	40.4
Percent Illegal/Criminal Aliens	11.9
Number of Pretrial Inmates Released Early per Month Due to Lack of Space	6,231
Number of Sentenced Inmates Released Early per Month Due to Lack of Space	5,922
Number of Inmates with 2 Strikes	3,016
Number of Inmates with 3 Strikes	1,476
Number of Medical Beds	948
Number of Mental Health Beds	3,493
Number of Assaults on Staff	274

SOURCE: California Board of Corrections, 2002. April to June 2002 Jail Profile Survey. Sacramento, CA: Available at http://www.bdcorr.ca.gov/fsod/jail%20profile%20summary/2002/quarter_2/pdf_files/ quarterly_summary_report.PDF.

610.7 per 100,000 were violent crimes with the remainder being property crimes.[27]

The population of prison inmates has also been increasing. From 1993 to 1998, the number of inmates going into the Department of Corrections system increased by 2.4 percent.[28] In 2002, the state of California had a prison inmate population of 75,602 (Average Daily Population) and a sizeable problem with overcrowding (see Table 2.5).

One factor often blamed for the increased prison population and overcrowding is the three strikes and you're out movement against habitual criminals. Following the 1993 kidnapping and murder of Polly Klaas from Petaluma, there came a growing outcry for stricter and harsher penalties and criminal justice laws. Following this call, California passed legislation stating that if an individual was found guilty of a felony after being found guilty of two earlier crimes, tougher penalties would be enforced—for the "third strike and you're out."

Subsequent to this legislation, the voters approved Proposition 184—the Three Strikes You're Out initiative, which went into effect on November 9, 1994. Proposition 184 set up strict requirements for the sentencing of third-strike candidates; these requirements stated that the third strike penalty would be the minimum of three times the sentence of each felony conviction, 25 years, or the term determined by the court—to be served in the state prison system. Significantly, these policies indicated that the third felony did not have to be a violent crime. However, two years later, the California Supreme Court gave sentencing discretion back to California to consider factors other than the number of crimes in determining sentences. Department of Corrections data indicate only 4,492 inmates in their system had either two or three strikes against them so the effects of Prop 184 are not a likely explanation for prison overcrowding. But this still does represent a significant number of individuals who were affected by the three strikes movement.

Sentencing discretion is also a concern when considering what many believe to be the inequitable and perhaps inaccurate application of the death penalty in California and elsewhere. Since 1977, eight individuals have been executed in California. Another 58 individuals on death row have been released, resentenced, or had their sentence overturned. There have been several cases nationally of individuals having their sentence overturned, given new evidence related to new technologies like DNA. In addition, of the 611 individuals currently on death row, 34.4 percent are African American and 19 percent are Hispanic American; this disproportionate racial and ethnic distribution provides evidence of a racially biased application of the death penalty. Many critics believe these incidents and the racial and ethnic imbalance among death row inmates suggest that continuing executions in California should be reconsidered.[29]

Several prominent cases, in California and elsewhere, such as the beating of Rodney King, captured on videotape; the shooting death in New York City of Amadou Diallo; highly publicized examples of racial profiling in police traffic stops; and the loss of credibility of the officers in the O.J. Simpson case, are putting police officers and the criminal justice system as a whole under the spotlight. Finally, a corruption scandal in the Los Angeles Rampart Division's anti-gang unit provided the impetus for a great deal of citizen organization around these issues in an attempt to reform the processes involved.

Incidents like these have the ultimate effect of undermining citizens' confidence in their police and criminal justice systems, which in turn often creates the perception of higher crime levels than actually exists in their communities.

HEALTH AND WELFARE

Health

California's population continues to age, and this has enormous impacts upon the state's health care system. In terms of prenatal care, childhood immunizations, and treatments of most cancers, there have been improvements in citizens' health care. Table 2.6 provides some indicators of the current health status of California's citizens.

Health care represents one of the central expenditures by individuals and by society as a whole. In 1996, health care spending represented approximately 12 percent of California's Gross State Product, over $137 billion per year, a steady increase since 1984.[30]

Table 2.6 California Health Status Indicators, 1999

Health Status Indicator	Status
Percentage of California Mothers Receiving Prenatal Care	80
Percentage of California Mothers Receiving Prenatal Care by End of Second Trimester	95
Percentage of Immunization Rate for 24-Month-Old Children	59
Infant Death Rate—1996 (One of lowest ever recorded)	5.9 per 1,000 live births
Deaths from Coronary Heart Disease	85.5 deaths per 100,000
Percentage of National Five-Year Breast Cancer Survival Rate	84
Incidence of Prostate Cancer in California (1995)	121.5 per 100,000
Lung Cancer Deaths in Women (1995)	33.1 per 100,000
Lung Cancer Deaths in Men (1995)	50.8 per 100,000
New Cases of AIDS Diagnosed in California (greatly declining)	6,341 cases

SOURCE: Office of Statewide Health Planning and Development, 1999. *California Health Care Fact Book*. Sacramento, California: Department of Health and Human Services.

Figure 2.1 shows the distribution of who paid these funds. Thirty-eight percent of the expenses are paid from public sources. These sources include Medicare, a federal program to pay the health care costs of the elderly and permanently disabled; federal Medicaid, a program to pay for the health care costs of the indigent; California's Medi-Cal program, funded by Federal Medicaid; and other public sources. Another 37 percent of health care payments come from private insurance sources while 18 percent come out of individuals' own pockets.[31]

Twenty to 25 percent of all Californians receive their health insurance through Medicare and Medi-Cal; these numbers steadily increased from 1988 to 1994, at which point the number of people enrolled peaked.[32] This reliance by so many upon the state for health care has important repercussions for the state budget, as health care is an expensive item.

One new program in California is the Healthy Families Program, which provides health care for children up to age 19 and for families who are not eligible for Medi-Cal, who have incomes that are 250 percent of federal poverty levels but who are not receiving health care coverage from other sources.

Still, one-quarter of all Californians are without health insurance; 40 percent of these citizens are working full-time and year-round but still cannot afford to purchase health insurance for themselves and their families.[33] The lack of health insurance for this large a population has enormous implications for the health care system as it struggles to pay for the rising costs of providing health care. Merely one catastrophic illness can bankrupt individuals without health insurance. The public sector ultimately ends up paying for uncovered costs.

The reality is that many of these patients cannot pay their medical bills, and the cost containment measures implemented by federal and state insurance pro-

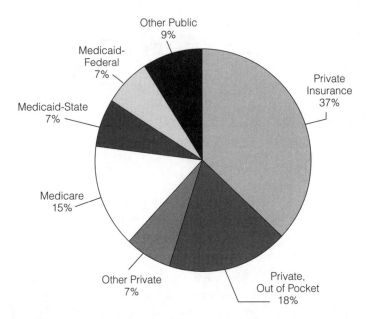

FIGURE 2.1. Health Care Expenditures by Payer Category (Percentage of Each Dollar Spent), 1999

SOURCE: Office of Statewide Health Planning and Development, 1999. *California Health Care Fact Book*. Sacramento, California: Department of Health and Human Services, p. 17.

grams have created problems for local public hospitals. They are being squeezed between increasing costs, uninsured patients who cannot pay their bills, and service reimbursement limits. The result is that hospitals are finding it increasingly hard to stay open and meet expenses.

Most Californians (63 percent) utilize health maintenance organizations (HMOs) for their health care.[34] Kaiser Foundation Health Plan is the largest in the state with 5.8 million members, followed by MedPartners, Blue Cross of California, HealthNet, and Pacificare. The top ten health care plans cover 21.9 million consumers.

Nationwide and statewide, the concentration of health care provision in the hands of so few private providers and the emergence of managed health care has caused enormous concern and consumer activism, leading to efforts to create a Patients Bill of Rights at the federal and other levels. In 1997 California passed SB 402, the California Pain Patients Bill of Rights, but broader protections have not yet passed.

Welfare

Not all of California's citizens are doing well financially. From 1980 to 1997, the percentage of individuals living below the poverty line in California steadily grew (see Figure 2.2)—from 11.0 in 1980 to 16.6 percent in 1997 but back

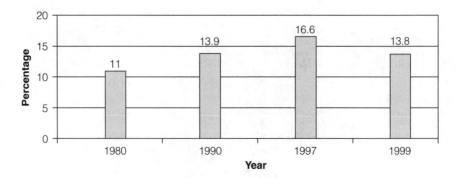

FIGURE 2.2. Percentage of Californians Living Below Poverty Level, 1980–1999

SOURCE: U.S. Census Bureau. 2001. Statistical Abstract of the United States. U.S. Department of Commerce, Table 684.

down to 13.8 in 1999; in 1997, there were 5.46 million Californians living in poverty, which was proportionately more than the 13.3 percent of the United States population as a whole who were living below the poverty line.[35] Another complication for California politics is that there is a large range of poverty levels across the state since income levels differ so extensively across the state; the proportion of individuals living under the poverty level ranges from the 5.2 percent in Marin County to the 23.8 percent in Imperial County. This variety means that state policies have to be developed to assist with very different situations.

The median income for the state in 1999 was $43,744, whereas the median income for the entire nation was $40,816; California ranked sixteenth in the nation in median income.[36] This inequality could perhaps be explained by two factors—the existence of more immigrants in the workforce and the greater premium that employers place on high skills and education levels.[37] Immigrants often have lower incomes because they do not enjoy, initially, higher education levels and related job skills. Meanwhile, those with high skills and advanced education have been able to cash in on the changes in the state's economy that have boosted industries like high tech, multimedia, entertainment, finance, and trade.[38] As a rapidly growing part of the labor force in California, immigrants' lower incomes significantly contribute to the income gap.

Ever since the beginning of the "welfare state" and social programs as we know them—during the New Deal in the 1930s and continuing through the War on Poverty in the 1960s—the role of the state in assisting those in poverty has been quite controversial. The most recent change resulted from a conservative push to ensure that individuals on grant assistance programs do not stay in those programs but instead move into the workforce quickly. In 1996, the Federal Aid to Families with Dependent Children program (AFDC) was replaced by the Temporary Assistance to Needy Families (TANF) through the

---

Class Exercise: Alternative Futures for California

Separate the class into groups. Have each group brainstorm on what California could look like in another ten years in each of the following areas: energy, environment, economy, transportation, education, diversity, and any other areas. Have each group describe three scenarios—the most optimistic, the most pessimistic, and the one in between those two options.

---

passage of the Personal Responsibility and Work Opportunity Reconciliation Act (PRWRA). Two years later, the California legislature passed legislation that implemented this program under the name of CalWorks (California Work Opportunity and Responsibility to Kids) Program. According to the California Department of Social Services, the guiding principles of the CalWorks Program are that individuals should not be on welfare for life; that they should work instead of being on welfare and exhibit personal responsibility to avoid rising rates of illegitimacy; and that welfare should not be granted for noncitizens and felons.[39]

During the initial periods of this program, an average of 707,018 cases were handled each month—for a total of $297 million up to September 1998.[40] The very magnitude of these amounts suggests that this new program is an important one for the state and its future and that the problem of poverty and social welfare lies squarely among the most intransigent issues facing California today.

REMAINING CHALLENGES

Poverty and welfare are clearly not alone in presenting significant challenges to the state of California for the immediate and long-term future. Many significant environmental and natural resource issues remain as the state moves into the 21st century. And there is the energy issue, which will be an important issue for some time.

Many of the remaining challenges are becoming more difficult to resolve precisely because of the growing population and congestion in California. These issues include the energy crisis, traffic congestion, mass transit (or lack of same), increasing loss of farmland, immigration issues, and many, many more.

What is clear is that Californians still have a chance to shape the future of their state, but only by educating themselves on the issues and by staying involved in their communities. These issues will not solve themselves. They are subject only to concentrated efforts and innovative, creative solutions.

ADDITIONAL RESOURCES

Public Policy Institute of California Web
site. Available at http://www.ppic.org.

Rand Institute Web site. Available at
http://www.rand.org.

State of California Web site. Available at
http://www.ca.gov.

NOTES

1. U.S. Department of Energy. 2001.
Background. Available at http://www.eia
.doe.gov/cneaf/electricity/california/
background.html.

2. Ibid.

3. California Energy Commission, 2001.
Power Plant Project Status. Available at
http://www.energy.ca.gov/sitingcases/
status_all_projects.html.

4. Lazarus, David. 2002. "Price-Fixing?
No Big Deal: Supplier Ignores the Evi-
dence." *San Francisco Chronicle,* A1, A22.
November 17, 2002; Federal Energy Reg-
ulatory Commission. 2002. Staff Fact-
Finding of Western Markets (Enron et al).
Available at http://www.ferc.fed.us/
electric/bulkpower/pa02-2/pa02-2.htm.

5. California Department of Finance.
2001. Budget Background Information—
Chart A: Historical Data, General Fund
Balance Sheet. Available at http://www
.dof.ca.gov/HTML/BUD_DOCS/
backinfo.htm.

6. U.S. Census Bureau, 1999. Poverty in
the United States: 1999. Washington,
DC.

7. Gray Davis, "Inaugural Address,"
January 4, 1999, www.state.ca.us/s/
governor/inauguraladdress.html.

8. U.S. Department of Education, State
Comparisons of Education Statistics:
1969–70 to 1996–97, Table 39.

9. EdData. 2002. Comparing California.
http://www.ed-data.k12.ca.us/
Navigation/fsTwoPanel.asp?bottom=/
snapshots/Snapshot.asp.

10. U.S. National Center for Education
Statistics. 2002. Mathematics Achieve-
ment-Level Results by State at Grade 8
Public Schools: 2000 in The Nation's

Report Card. Department of Education,
Available at http://nces.ed.gov/nations
reportcard/mathematics/results/
stateachieve-g8.asp.

11. Ibid.

12. California Secretary of Education,
http://www.ose.ca.gov/api/index.html.

13. California Department of Finance,
State Budget 2000–2001 Highlights.

14. California Postsecondary Education
Commission, "Higher Education Enroll-
ment Demand," http://www.cpec.ca.gov/
PressRelease/EnrTables.htm.

15. Rand Corporation. 1998. *Breaking the
Social Contract: The Fiscal Crisis in Califor-
nia Higher Education.* Rand: Santa Monica,
CA.

16. California State University. CSU
Enrollment for Fall 2001. Available at
http://www.calstate.edu/PA/info/
enroll.shtml.

17. Public Policy Institute of California,
2002. PPIC Statewide Survey: Special
Survey on Californians and the Environment. San Francisco: Public Policy Institute of California, June 2002. Available
at http://www.ppic.org/publications/
CalSurvey28/survey28.pdf.

18. Rachel Carson, *Silent Spring* (Green-
wich, CT: Fawcett, 1962).

19. California Department of Finance,
2000. California: An Economic Profile.
Sacramento: California Department of
Finance.

20. Ibid.

21. California Department of Water Resources. 1998. Bulletin 160-98: California
Water Plan. Sacramento, California: Division of Planning and Local Assistance,
Department of Water Resources.

22. California Department of Water Resources. 2000. California's Water Future: A Framework for Action.

23. California Environmental Protection Agency. 1998. U.C. Report on MTBE: Health and Environmental Assessment of MTBE—Report to the Governor and Legislature—Fact Sheet http://tsrtp.ucdavis.edu/mtberpt/mtbefact.pdf.

24. U.S. Environmental Protection Agency. 2002. U.S. EPA: Emissions Tracking System (ETS) Preliminary Cumulative Values for 2002, Through Quarter 3 Report for California. Washington, D.C.: U.S. Environmental Protection Agency Acid Rain Program, Available at http://www.epa.gov/airmarkets/emissions/prelimarp/02q3/023_ca.txt.

25. California Air Resources Board. 1999. ARB Almanac 1999. Sacramento: California, Air Resources Board, Figure 2-1.

26. Criminal Justice Statistics Center, 2000. Criminal Statistics. Criminal Justice Statistics Center, Available at http://caag.state.ca.us/cjsc.

27. Criminal Justice Statistics Center, 2000. Table 11: California Crime Index, 1999. Criminal Justice Statistics Center, available at http://justice.hdcdojnet.state.ca.us/cjsc_stats/prof99/00/11.pdf.

28. Criminal Justice Statistics Center, 2000. Table 47: Adults Committed to State Institutions, 1993–1998. Criminal Justice Statistics Center, available at

http://caag.state.ca.us/cjsc/cd98/tabs/cd98tb47.pdf.

29. Death Penalty Focus, 2000. Facts: California Death Row Statistics. Available at http://208.55.30.156/facts/other/facts_statistics.shtml.

30. Office of Statewide Health Planning and Development, 1999. California Health Care Fact Book. Sacramento: California Department of Health and Human Services, 16.

31. Ibid., 17.

32. Ibid., 22.

33. Ibid., 24.

34. Ibid., 20.

35. U.S. Census Bureau. 2001. Statistical Abstract of the United States. U.S. Department of Commerce, Table 684.

36. Ibid., Table 667.

37. *San Francisco Chronicle,* "Gap Reported Wider Between Rich, Poor," February 9, 1999, A15.

38. Ibid.

39. California Department of Social Services. 1998. Temporary Assistance for Needy Families: A Characteristics Survey on the Social and Economic Characteristics of Families Receiving Aid. Sacramento: California Department of Social Services, 1.

40. Ibid., 2.

3

Political Parties and Interest Group Politics

Consider the case of Audie Bock, a Green Party activist from Piedmont (Alameda County) who became the first member of the California State Assembly elected from the Green Party, becoming the only member of the state legislature who was not Democrat or Republican and the very first member of the Green Party ever elected to the legislature. Before the first year was over, however, she had transferred her party registration to Independent. Before she completed her first term and left office (she did not run again for a second term), she had transferred her registration to Democratic. Why? Without affiliation or support from a major party, the difficulties in achieving any kind of policy impact were so great that an assembly member who was not a party member had very little chance of having an impact. The two parties control how the assembly and state senate are organized—along with committee assignments, policy priorities, and day-to-day allocation of resources. As Bock stated, "It is difficult for her to play a major role in any issue area because, under the terms of a bipartisan agreement, the Democrats, who control both houses of the California legislature, chair all committees, and Republicans, as the minority, are given the vice chair slots."[1] So members elected as Independents or from a party other than Democrat or Republican find themselves on the outside, unable to have any meaningful impact upon California politics or policies. And so went the election of the first Green Party member to the California legislature.

POLITICAL PARTIES IN CALIFORNIA

Political parties in California hold a different role in voters' minds than in many other states. The two major parties, Democrats and Republicans, each enroll more than 5 million potential voters, but Californians have turned in increasing numbers to alternative parties like the Green Party, Reform Party, and others.

Party registration figures for the November 2002 election (see Table 3.1) indicate that the Democratic Party holds the most registrations across the state (44.6 percent), followed by the 35.21 percent for the Republican Party (or, the Grand Ole Party—GOP).[2] The American Independent, Green, and Libertarian parties were the next three largest parties, followed by the Natural Law and Reform parties. The profile of Californians who were willing to vote for a third-party candidate cuts across regional, racial, gender, income, and educational lines.

Figure 3.1 shows the changes in the proportions of voters registered for each party across three decades of California politics. Including just the voters who have registered as Democratic, Republican, or Independent (those who declined to state a party preference or who did not declare for a listed party, but declared miscellaneous), the trends are clear. Registration for the Democratic Party is still growing but at a declining rate, and this party still holds by far the most dominant position in the state. The GOP experienced large growth in registration in the 1980s and slight growth since then. The other, minor parties listed above have maintained or experienced slight declines—there have been no large increases for any of these parties. Since California's population has grown, the number of Republican voters has also grown—3,274,967 voters in 1970 to 5,388,895 in 2002.[3]

The biggest change in political party affiliation has been in the proportion of voters who consider themselves Independents. In 1970, there were only 278,284 of these, but by 2002 that number had increased practically nine times—to 2,440,453, or 15.9 percent of registered voters.[4]

The profile of the average voter changes significantly according to party (see Table 3.2). Independent voters are significantly younger (42 percent are 18 to 34 years old) and a greater percentage is male (57 percent) than those voters registered elsewhere. Democratic voters tend to be significantly older (30 percent are 55 and older) than independents. In addition, a greater percentage of Democratic voters are Latino (25 percent), African American (10 percent), and female (58 percent) than are the voters of other parties. A larger percentage of Republican voters than for other parties are white (81 percent) with fewer (18 percent) having no college education at all.[5]

There are also significant regional differences among the parties (see Figure 3.2). Orange County and the Inland Empire areas contain significantly more Republican voters while the Central Valley is almost evenly mixed. Both Los Angeles and the San Francisco Bay Area contain a majority of Democratic voters with significantly fewer Republicans. Independents and voters from other parties are almost evenly represented across the state.[6]

Table 3.1 California Political Party Voter Registration, October 21, 2002

Registration	Number of Voters	Percentage of Total Registered Voters
Total Eligible	21,466,274	—
Total Registered	15,303,469	—
Democratic Party	6,825,400	44.6
Republican Party	5,388,895	35.21
American Independent	299,231	1.96
Green Party	155,952	1.02
Libertarian Party	90,495	0.59
Natural Law Party	44,561	0.29
Reform Party	58,482	0.38
Miscellaneous	119,945	0.78

SOURCE: California Secretary of State. Available at http://www.ss.ca.gov/ elections/ror/county_10-21-02.pdf.

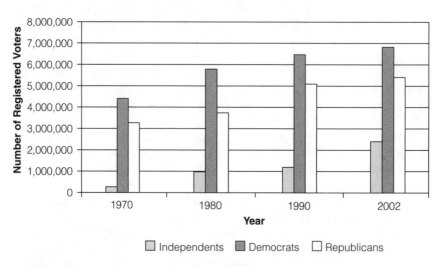

FIGURE 3.1. Party Registration Trends for Major Parties, 1970–2002

SOURCES: Table 3-1. Mark Baldassare. 2000. *California in the New Millennium: The Changing Social and Political Landscape*. Berkeley: University of California Press in conjunction with the Public Policy Institute of California, 62; and California Secretary of State's Office, 2002. Report of Registration as of October 21, 2002. Registration by County Secretary of State. Available at http://www.ss.ca.gov/elections/ror/county_10-21-02.pdf.

These party differences according to individual characteristics and region mean that the political parties and individual candidates have to devise appropriate strategies for attracting voters to their positions and their candidacies. These differences can also lead to very divisive campaigns, as the interests of one region are often very different from the interests of another. Campaigns that

A Closer Look

Are you currently registered to vote? Under which party, or as an independent? How about your friends and family? Ask your friends and family who have been involved in civic affairs the longest period of time about their party affiliation. Have they changed their party registration or affiliation over the past years— why or why not?

Table 3.2 Demographic Profile of California Voters, 1998

Characteristic	Independents	Democrats	Republicans
Age			
18–34	42%	26%	23%
35–54	41	44	43
55 and older	17	30	34
Education			
College Graduate	41	36	44
Some College	34	34	38
Less: (No) College Education	25	30	18
Race/Ethnicity			
White	66	59	81
Latino	19	25	11
Black	5	10	1
Asian/Other	10	6	7
Gender			
Men	57	42	49
Women	43	58	51

SOURCE: Table 3-2. Mark Baldassare. 2000. *California in the New Millennium: The Changing Social and Political Landscape.* Berkeley: University of California Press with the Public Policy Institute of California, 65.

appeal to one group or region will undoubtedly leave another region out. For instance, former Governor Wilson placed reforms in immigration and affirmative action at the forefront of his last campaign. This appeal to more conservative voters offended more progressive voters and voters of color. Thus, the extreme differences between the parties seen here do not bode well for consensus on California public policy and political issues in the future.

Qualifying to Be on the Ballot

How does a political party qualify to be on the ballot in California? State election law allows for two methods: signing up 86,212 (the number needed in 2002) new party members through voter registration or gathering 862,113 signatures

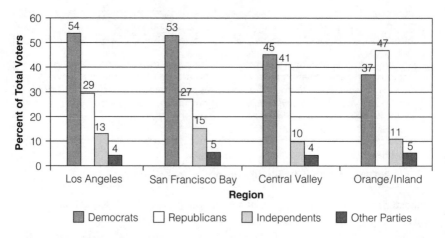

FIGURE 3.2. Party Voter Registration by Region, 1998

SOURCE: Table 5-3. Mark Baldassare. 2000. *California in the New Millennium: The Changing Social and Political Landscape.* Berkeley: University of California Press in conjunction with the Public Policy Institute of California, 149.

A Closer Look

Investigate party affiliations in your own area by going to the Web site for the California secretary of state (http://www.ss.ca.gov/elections/ elections_u.htm) and downloading the most recent report on county-level party registration. What impact do these party registrations have on the political campaigns in your area? How might the political campaigning, political ads, and policy issues that are emphasized be different if there were different party affiliations or different demographic groups represented in your area?

of registered voters on petitions—or 10 percent of all voters voting, in this case, in the November 1998 general election. However, organizers of a potential political party must first hold a party caucus, draft a party platform, and pick a name for their party before they can seek sufficient signatures to qualify the party for the ballot.

Two alternative parties—the Reform Party and the Peace and Freedom Party—did not garner enough votes in the 1998 election to remain on the ballot in 2000 because they failed to get more than 2 percent of the vote in the previous election. Both parties had until October 24, 1999, to prove to the state that they had at least the 86,176 registered voters in their parties necessary to return to the ballot in 2000. Both parties successfully met that deadline. The Peace and Freedom Party has been on the state ballot since 1968. It was founded in 1967 as an anti-war party. The Reform Party, an offshoot of Texas billionaire Ross Perot's first presidential bid in 1992, qualified for the ballot in 1995.

Party Structure

State law clearly mandates how political parties are to be structured, with minor differences in the two major party organizations. The basic structure of political parties in California includes:

> National Committee members
>
> Delegates to the National Party Conventions
>
> County Central Committees
>
> State Central Committees
>
> State Party chairs
>
> State Party Conventions

Figure 3.3 describes the relationships between these different party entities, using the California Democratic Party structure as an example. All of these organizational units are described below.

National Committee Members. National Committee members are elected by the party's delegation to the national convention and serve as the state party's representatives on each party's national committee. They meet on a periodic basis with National Committee members from other states and serve as the policy-makers for the national parties.

Delegates to the National Convention. Supporters of each candidate who is running in the party primaries develop slates of party convention delegates. The winning delegates—with alterations and additions—go to the national conventions and cast the state's votes at the party presidential conventions. In California, Republicans use the so-called winner-take-all primary, where the winner gains all of the available delegates. State Democrats rely upon a proportional representation system of delegates elected from congressional districts; this means that each candidate wins the number of delegates equal to their proportion of votes won.

State and National Party Platforms. At both the state and national levels, parties develop their party platforms. Platforms are statements of purpose and views on various policy issues; they state what the parties stand for. Ideally, they provide a statement of principles on which party candidates base their campaigns, although in reality, candidates rarely feel compelled to confine themselves to their party's platform.

County Central Committees. County Central Committees are elected directly by the voters and are charged with directing party affairs in each county. In fact, however, these committees are weak, with the real power being held by the officeholders in each county.

State Central Committees. These committees comprise party members from the different political parties who are the decision-makers and policy-makers in each party. They are charged with electing party officials to manage

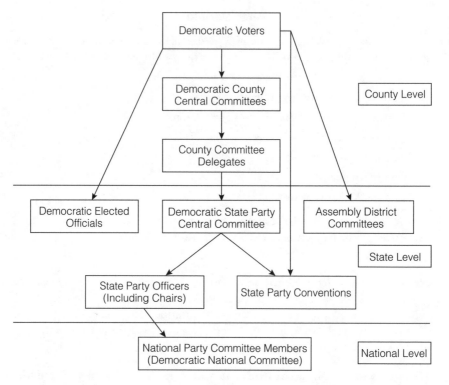

FIGURE 3.3. Example of Party Structure: California Democratic Party

SOURCE: Based on California Democratic Party. 2002. About Party Structure. Available at http://www.ca-dem.org/party_structure.php.

the party and select presidential electors. An executive committee of the state central committee handles the day-to-day operations of the party.

State Chairs. In theory, state chairs speak for the party and develop election strategy in conjunction with the executive committee. With rare exceptions, however, the main leaders are the major officeholders of both parties.[7]

State Party Conventions. State party conventions are also held to develop party platforms, hear candidates speak, and conduct party business. They are held every two years in advance of state elections.

Changes in California Primary Elections

Primaries are the elections where political party members (voters registered for each party) vote to elect their party's nominees to political office. There are two types of primaries—and several variations on these themes. A closed primary requires that voters vote only for candidates of their own primary.

The open primary allows voters to vote for candidates of any party, no matter in which party the voter is registered. A Republican may vote for a Democrat and a Democrat may vote for a candidate from the Green or Reform Party. Open primaries allow individuals to vote for whoever they feel is the best-qualified candidate, regardless of party affiliation. Unfortunately, it also adversely affects political parties and aids in their gradual decline because voters feel less and less tied to their party and focus, instead, more on individual candidates. Some voters also have tried to help out the candidate of their choice by voting for a candidate from another party whom they consider to be the weaker candidate, although there is little evidence of the effectiveness of this strategy. They therefore attempt to set up the weaker candidate to run against their own and so help to ensure their candidate's success.

Due to a voter approved change in the 1996 Proposition 198, California moved to open primaries rather than closed primaries. The 2000 presidential election was the first presidential election in which the open primary was utilized, but the courts then changed this system.

In 1996, another change occurred—California's primary and the presidential primary were moved ahead on the calendar to the fourth Tuesday in March 1996 to give California voters a greater opportunity to influence presidential nomination politics. Many states have moved their primary dates, creating a "musical chairs" effect as they all attempt to be the first primary and influence the presidential nominee selection process.

How Important Are Political Parties?

Political parties in California have not been particularly strong since the days of Hiram Johnson and the Progressive movement that began in 1911. As in the rest of the country, they are steadily declining in importance.

Prior to their weakening, parties served as a handy guide to elections. Voters could vote for their party candidates and platform positions rather than having to make individual selections of each candidate and position.

Parties are crucial to the average person, who is confronted with a task that staggers the most alert citizen—to learn enough political information to make informed decisions at the voting booth. As parties have lost their connection to citizens, most today pick up their civic information in a haphazard way. At the same time, television and other media have grown in importance. This leaves voters to screen through the barrage of information that comes at them from many different types of political advertising. Those candidates who are most effective in manipulating the media have an advantage over those less adroit in these matters—particularly in the television age.

Interest groups and political public relation firms have filled the vacuum created by the shrinking party by taking advantage of this need for information and by attempting to influence public opinion. Purposeful, well organized, and well financed, they influence both campaigns and actions in the legislature. Rather than rely upon assistance from their parties, as was the case in the past, candidates rely upon their own campaign organizations and interest groups to reach the public and to raise campaign funds.

CALIFORNIA INTEREST GROUPS

Interest groups are voluntary associations of individuals or groups banding together to forward some common interest. In California, interest groups have moved to fill much of the void in political power left by the declining political parties.

The theory that explains political interest group influence in the political and policy process is called pluralism. Under this theory, groups help to create public policy by bargaining and compromising with one another to achieve desired ends. Political and policy outcomes tend to be compromises achieved between the groups involved in an issue.

Prior to the 1970s and 1980s, creating compromise was not typically the role of interest groups, but of political parties. Parties helped achieve policy goals and keep the political system stable by providing one place for interest groups to join together with at least some shared values and goals. Because of these shared views, groups were able to achieve the compromises needed to successfully reach their policy goals—and parties were important to achieving those compromises.

During the 1970s and 1980s, the power of political action committees (PACs) had begun to emerge and political parties were declining. The emergence of these PACs, or organized committees that could legally contribute money to candidates, helped the development of interest group power as candidates went directly to the interest groups to get campaign help and assistance.

Interest groups include representatives from the following types of organizations:

- Public interest groups
- Economic issue groups
- Single-issue groups
- Demographic groups
- Professional associations
- Unions

Organizations such as the Sierra Club, Consumers Union, and Public Citizen are known as public interest groups. Traditionally, these groups have limited financial resources; interest groups influence legislation through argument and education and tactics such as letter-writing campaigns, petitions, issues research, and individual lobbying. Not all public interest groups are directly involved in elections. Some maintain (and advertise) lists of legislators most friendly to their causes. They sponsor PACs that contribute funds to chosen candidates. PACs usually support a wide variety of issues.

Southern California Public Power Authority, the Coalition of California Independent Refineries and Terminals, and Exxon Mobil Corporation are examples of economic issue groups, groups that organize both individually and collectively to advance their economic interests. These organizations typically employ full-time lobbyists who work for their interests in the state capitol, contribute funds to candidates (often candidates from all major parties to avoid offending any one candidate who might win), and advertise widely to build support for their positions.

Single-issue groups tend to utilize the same type of strategies as the PACs but focus only on one issue. Examples of single-issue groups include Handgun Control, the National Rifle Association (NRA), Operation Rescue, and the National Association of Reform of Abortion Laws (NARAL). Because they are typically not willing to compromise and bargain with other groups, the political system sometimes comes to a halt around these issues when the negotiation and compromise needed to achieve results is not possible.

Professional associations and unions represent individuals based upon their work roles and the interests of their professions and organizations. The California Teachers Association, the California Nursing Association, and the California Fire Chiefs Association are examples of these types of organizations. While most of these groups do not have the extensive financial resources of the economic interest groups against which they are frequently fighting, some, including the California Medical Association and the California Teachers Association, wield significant economic power. However, even the financially weak organizations frequently have the power of numbers—the numbers of their members who are willing to be politically active and write letters, lobby their legislators, sign petitions, and vote.

Demographic groups work for the interests of some individual group of citizens who band together based upon their common interests and characteristics. Examples include the NAACP (the National Association for the Advancement of Colored People) and MALDEF (the Mexican American Legal Defense Educational Fund). Like public interest groups, these groups tend not to have much money and so focus instead upon strategies that can take advantage of their larger numbers of voters.

Lobbying Expenditures

Each of these types of groups uses lobbying techniques (attempts to influence the political or policy process through education and persuading legislators of their views) and seeks to elect legislators who are sympathetic to their views. The amount of money spent in the state of California on lobbying—attempting to influence the actions of either the state legislators or state administrative processes—is enormous—over $212 million![8]

The level of lobbying expenditures is one indicator of the power that is used to influence the political process. While these expenditures do not represent attempts to buy votes, they do represent money used during the political process to educate, inform, and even help write legislation.

A Closer Look

Do you belong to any interest groups? Do you pay membership dues to any groups? What political activities do the groups to which you belong engage? What issues are they fighting for? Find their Web sites and use them to determine the political strategies used by these groups to attempt to influence the political process. How aware were you and your fellow members of the issues being emphasized and the strategies being employed?

Table 3.3 California Lobbying Expenditures January 1, 1999–March 30, 2000 (Ranked from Highest to Lowest Expenditures)

Category of Lobbying Groups	Expenditures
Government Groups	$31,935,995
Health	25,979,275
Miscellaneous	24,351,966
Manufacturing/Industrial	20,468,931
Finance and Insurance	19,944,453
Education	17,561,666
Professional/Trade	12,171,462
Utilities	11,425,609
Oil and Gas	8,379,996
Labor Unions	7,967,408
Real Estate	5,943,695
Agriculture	4,439,809
Transportation	4,131,823
Legal	3,876,687
Public Employees	3,455,697
Merchandising/Retail	3,437,841
Lodging/Restaurants	1,049,376
Political Organizations	364,603
Total Expenditures	$212,280,660

SOURCE: California Secretary of State. 2000. *Overview of Lobbying Expenditures, January 1999–March 2000.* Sacramento: Office of California Secretary of State.

As an example of the types of money raised and groups that are participating in this process, Table 3.3 presents data on the lobbying expenditures made by different categories of interest groups from January 1, 1999, until March 30, 2000.

Government groups spent the most (practically $32 million) during this period, followed by health groups, miscellaneous, manufacturing/industrial,

**Table 3.4 Top Ten California Lobbyist Employers January 1, 1999–
March 30, 2000 (Ranked from Highest to Lowest Expenditures)**

Lobbyist Employers	Cumulative Expenditures
California Teachers Association	$4,397,338
Pacific Telesis Group and subsidiaries	2,695,608
Western States Petroleum Association	2,557,330
State Farm Insurance Companies	2,100,144
Nature Conservancy Inc.	1,830,490
California Healthcare Association and related entities	1,789,093
Edison International and subsidiaries	1,734,258
California Chamber of Commerce	1,721,245
California Manufacturers Association	1,700,355
California Medical Association Inc.	1,678,350

SOURCE: California Secretary of State. 2000. *Overview of Lobbying Expenditures, January 1999–March 2000.*
Sacramento: Office of California Secretary of State.

finance and insurance, education, professional/trade, utilities, oil and gas, and labor unions. Note the number of these groups that are economic issue groups and professional associations, protecting the economic interests of companies, industries, or individuals.

The power of these groups is further illustrated by Table 3.4, which lists the expenditures for lobbying employers, the companies actually paying the lobbyists. This data indicates the expenditures by individual companies and groups rather than by category. The California Teachers Association leads this list with expenditures of $4,397,338, followed by the Pacific Telesis Group with practically $2.7 million, the Western States Petroleum Association with practically $2.6 million, and the State Farm Insurance agencies with $2.1 million. Next on the list is the Nature Conservancy, having spent $1.8 million during that period.[9]

PARTIES AND INTEREST
GROUPS IN CALIFORNIA

In California, as in the rest of the nation, parties are declining in importance and interest groups are growing in importance and influence. Both parties and interest groups have important roles to play in the political system; as these roles change, so does the system itself. To date, no one knows exactly what is emerging in the near and far future. What role remains for ordinary citizens? Who will have power in the future? Answers to these questions are emerging as we speak and study.

A Closer Look

Audie Bock might not have been elected even ten years earlier, when parties were stronger—voters might not have chosen to go with an unknown activist who represented the Green Party. And still, Ms. Bock chose to change her party affiliation to Independent from Green. What does that say about the importance of parties and party affiliation?

ADDITIONAL RESOURCES

Baldassare, Mark. 2000. *California in the New Millennium: The Changing Social and Political Landscape.* Berkeley: University of California Press and the Public Policy Institute of California.

California Secretary of State Web site. http://www.ss.ca.gov.

California Secretary of State Elections Information. http://www.ss.ca.gov/elections/elections.htm.

California AFL-CIO Web site. http://www.calaborfed.org.

Democratic Party of California Web site. http://www.ca-dem.org.

Green Party of California Web site. http://www.cagreens.org.

Republican Party of California Web site. http://www.cagop.org.

NOTES

1. Institute of Governmental Studies. 1999. Public Affairs Report. Available at http://www.igs.berkeley.edu:8880/publications/par/Sept1999/Bock.html.

2. California Secretary of State. 2000. Party Registrations. Available at http://www.ss.ca.gov/elections/ror/ county_10-00.pdf.

3. Mark Baldassare. 2000. *California in the New Millennium: The Changing Social and Political Landscape.* Berkeley: University of California Press in conjunction with the Public Policy Institute of California, Table 3-1, pp. 62; California Secretary of State. 2002. Report of Registration as of October 21, 2002. Registration by County. Available at http://www.ss.ca .gov/elections/ror/county_10-21-02.pdf.

4. Mark Baldassare. 2000. *California in the New Millennium: The Changing Social and Political Landscape.* Berkeley: University of California Press in conjunction with the Public Policy Institute of California, Table 3-1, 62.

5. Ibid.,Table 3-2, 65.

6. Ibid.,Table 5-3, 149.

7. Thomas R. Hoeber and Charles M. Price, eds., *California Government and Politics Annual 1995–1996* (Sacramento, CA: Journal Press, 1995), 50.

8. California Secretary of State. 2000. Overview of Lobbying Expenditures, January 1999–March 2000. Sacramento: Office of California Secretary of State, iii.

9. Ibid., v.

4

The Electoral Process, Money, the Media, and the Internet

Elections in California have an impact that ranges far beyond the actual borders of the state. In the 2000 presidential elections, California's 54 electoral votes were the holy grail of all the presidential candidates (they were 20 percent of the votes needed to win the election). With Al Gore, George W. Bush, and Ralph Nader all inspiring contingents of support among state voters, some interesting schemes emerged. Some voters wanted to vote for Ralph Nader but did not want to hand the election to Bush by switching their vote away from Gore. Prior to the election, it appeared possible that Nader could draw enough votes in California to make that happen. In other states, the opposite was true—voters could safely vote for Nader without that vote potentially making any difference. The digital age response? Several Web sites emerged that allowed the Nader voters from California to switch their Nader votes into Gore votes, trading with Gore voters in other states who subsequently voted for Nader. Upon investigation, California Secretary of State Bill Jones required that the offending sites be shut down, citing laws that outlawed the purchase of any vote with anything of value, and effectively ending this new twist on voting and the Internet.

This chapter will highlight the various types of elections that occur in California, will discuss who votes in California, and will highlight the impact that money and the media—and, now, the Internet—have on California elections.

ELECTORAL PROCESS IN CALIFORNIA

California is known for its sometimes strange and always interesting elections. One reason California elections are rarely dull is the rich variety of choices voters are given, in the form of local and statewide initiatives and offbeat as well as mainstream political parties. The disadvantage for California voters is the long and complex ballot, full of numerous state and local ballot measures that they must navigate.

People usually associate elections with party politics. However, nearly all of the more than nineteen thousand elected offices (federal, state, and local) in California are nonpartisan. Candidates do not identify themselves by party label or represent a political party when they run for a *nonpartisan* office, whereas in *partisan* elections candidates are first nominated for office in their parties' primaries.

Several types of elections typically occur in California (and in other states, too)—primary, general, and runoffs.

Primary Elections

Primaries are held in even-numbered years to select party candidates for state, federal, and some local offices. Prior to the 1996 presidential primary, California held its party primaries on the first Tuesday after the first Monday in June. However, by holding its primary elections so late in the presidential primary season, California effectively gave up its enormous political power in helping to decide the Democratic and Republican parties presidential candidates since so many delegates had already been determined. In 1996, California experimented with holding its primary elections on the fourth Tuesday in March, but this experiment failed to improve California's position relative to other states simply because they too moved up their primary elections.

Determined to have a major voice in the selection of future presidential candidates, California established the first Tuesday in March as its primary election date beginning with the 2000 elections. This means that, effectively, the entire nominating process could take less than a month from start to finish: from the Iowa caucuses and New Hampshire primary in February, to a welter of potentially decisive contests including California and New York in early March, to a possible tie-breaker in the South on "Super Tuesday." Lamar Alexander, the former education secretary and Tennessee governor who ran for president in 1996 and 2000, said that when he ran, he thought of "Iowa as the launching pad, New Hampshire as the semifinals, and March 7 [2000] looks like the settler, with California having the biggest voice on that day."[1]

General Elections

On the first Tuesday after the first Monday in November in even-numbered years, general elections are held. Unlike primary elections, ballots in the general election do not vary by party. Voters can select from among all candidates, including those nominated by the political party in the March primary and

Table 4.1 Presidential Candidates on the General Election, November 7, 2000, California Ballot (By Number of Votes Cast)

Presidential Candidate	Party Affiliation	Percent of General-Population Vote
Al Gore, *President* Joe Lieberman, *Vice President*	Democratic Party	53.5 (5,861,203 votes)
George W. Bush, *President* Dick Cheney, *Vice President*	Republican Party	41.7 (4,567,4 29)
Ralph Nader, *President* Winona Laduke, *Vice President*	Green Party	3.9 (418,707)
Harry Browne, *President* Art Olivier, *Vice President*	Libertarian Party	0.4 (45,520)
Patrick J. Buchanan, *President* Ezola Foster, *Vice President*	Reform Party	0.4 (44,987)
Howard Phillips, *President* J. Curtis Frazier, *Vice President*	American Independent Party	0.1 (17,042)
John Hagelin, *President* Nat Goldhaber, *Vice President*	Natural Law Party	0.0 (10,934)

SOURCE: Secretary of State's Office.

Table 4.2 Gubernatorial Candidates on the General Election, November 5, 2002, California Ballot (By Number of Votes Cast)

Candidate Gubernatorial	Party Affiliation	Percent of General-Population Vote
Gray Davis	Democratic Party	47.4 (3,469,025 votes)
Bill Simon	Republican Party	42.4 (3,105,477)
Reinhold Gulke	American Independent Party	1.7 (125,338)
Peter Miguel Camejo	Green Party	5.3 (381,700)
Gary David Copeland	Libertarian Party	2.1 (158,161)
Iris Adam	Natural Law Party	1.1 (86,432)

SOURCE: Secretary of State's Office.

those filed as independents (see Table 4.1 for the candidates on the presidential ballot in California in 2000 and the state results of those elections).

Table 4.2 shows the results of the November 2002 gubernatorial elections in California, when Governor Gray Davis was re-elected after a fierce battle with Republican challenger Bill Simon. In that controversial race, Davis had unleashed a series of negative ads prior to the March primary against Republican Richard Reardon, widely considered the strongest Republican candidate.

Table 4.3 Ballot Initiatives on the General Election, November 5, 2002, California Ballot (By Number of Yes Votes Cast)

Proposition Number	Proposition Name	Percentage (and Number) of Yes Votes (Whether Passed or Not)
46	Housing and Emergency Shelter Trust Fund	57.6 (3,984,920 votes)
47	Kindergarten–University Facilities Bond	59.1 (4,139,600)
48	Court Consolidation	72.9 (4,751,568)
49	After School Programs, State Grants	56.7 (3,947,249)
50	Water Quality, Supply/ Safe Drinking Water Bonds	55.4 (3,809,259)
51*	Transportation, Allocation of Motor Vehicle Taxes	41.4 (2,775,226)
52*	Election Day Voter Registration	40.5 (2,808,818)

SOURCE: California Secretary of State's Office.

*These propositions did not pass.

California voters also choose whether or not to support a series of ballot propositions, policy issues that can be approved by the voters. Ballots in the general election are very long because there are numerous initiatives and referendums (see Table 4.3 for a list of the ballot initiatives on the November 5, 2002, ballot and the results of those elections) and a great many elected offices at the state and local levels, including judgeships.

If there has not been a clear winner with a majority of the votes, then runoff elections are held to allow voters to decide between the top two vote-getters. Runoff elections are typically used in local elections but have a major problem in that voter turnout declines significantly after the general election.

Open Primaries

In the March 1996 elections, nearly 60 percent of the voters in California approved the "open primary" system when they voted for Proposition 198. The open primary allowed voters to cross party lines to cast their ballots—to vote for candidates of a party other than their own. Instead of Democratic voters being restricted to voting only for Democratic candidates and Republican voters for Republican candidates, and so forth, voters had the opportunity to vote for any candidate regardless of their party affiliation. The party candidate receiving the most votes running for a particular office was listed as that party's nominee on the general election ballot. Republican and Democratic county central committee members, however, were elected on a separate party ballot available only to their respective party voters.

The open primary replaced the "closed primary" that dated back to the early 20th century, when Progressive reformers successfully promoted it to undercut domination of the nominating slates at state conventions. Those opposed to the open primary argued that it would weaken the political parties in California. They also feared that the open primary would blur the ideological differences between candidates and the major political parties, forcing candidates to move even further to the center. In critics' minds, this would be unhealthy for political debate and the electoral process. Those favoring the open primary believed it would encourage higher voter turnout because the open primary would enable minority party registrants a greater opportunity to influence election outcomes. In fact, more people voted in the June 1998 primary—the first open primary—than had in many years.

In June 2000 the United States Supreme Court declared California's open primary unconstitutional, ruling that it violated the right of free association with a political party. Today, California has a modified closed primary system—voters not affiliated with a party may participate in a party primary under certain conditions.

Other Types of Elections

Special elections are held to take care of special situations, such as when a vacancy needs to be filled, or a special ballot measure must be decided before the next regular election. When possible, special circumstances requiring voter approval are combined with regularly scheduled elections to save voter time and taxpayer money.

A special election to fill a vacancy in state and congressional offices or to determine a statewide issue (except for bond measures) may be called by the governor. At the local level, "the governing body of a county, city, or school district may call a special election to fill a vacancy or vote on a bond act, charter question, or other ballot measure."[2] Even though the issues or elective offices featured in a special election are rather important, even fewer voters turn out at the polls during these elections because they tend to be much less visible and less publicized in the media and by activists.

California voters also have the power to remove any state or local government official from office—in a special recall election. A petition asking for a recall election must be first circulated for signatures of qualified voters. For statewide officers, there must be a number of signatures of registered voters at least equivalent to 12 percent of the last vote for the office gathered in at least five counties. For members of the state senate or assembly and members of the state judiciary, the number of signatures must equal 20 percent of the last vote.[3]

The petition must state the reason for the recall—any reason will do. If sufficient signatures are gathered, then an election is held to decide two questions: should the incumbent be removed from office, and, if so, who should succeed that person to office?[4]

A Closer Look

Go to http://www.ss.ca.gov/elections/ elections_r.htm and find out who are your representatives to the state assembly, state senate, and U.S. House of Representatives. Now, go to http://Vote2002.ss.ca.gov/Returns.htm and find out how much of the vote they won in the general election on election day (November 5) 2002.

VOTING IN CALIFORNIA

There are very few restrictions on who can vote in California. People are eligible to vote if they are at least 18 years of age, U.S. citizens, and residents of California. The only people not eligible to vote are prison inmates, those on parole for having committed a felony, or those deemed to be mentally incompetent.[5]

The registration process is fairly easy in California. One need only to mail a completed registration form, which is available at the post office as well as at the many voter drives conducted at shopping malls, at community centers, on college campuses, and in churches. The process was made even easier with the passage of the "motor voter" law. This law provides more locations at which a voter can register, including the Department of Motor Vehicles and various other government offices.

However, another proposed change to the election system, to allow voters to register on the day of the election (Proposition 52 on the November 2002 ballot), was not passed. Many evidently felt that would make voting too easy and could lead to possible fraud and administrative problems.

Once Californians are registered to vote, they need not register again unless they move to another county. The first time people register it is necessary to do so at least 29 days before an election in which they plan to vote. If a voter moves to another address within the same county, it is necessary only to request from the county clerk a special postage-paid address correction card.

A growing number of people are choosing to vote absentee. Any registered voters may apply for an absentee ballot, and it is no longer necessary to provide a reason for wanting to vote absentee. Today, it is a common strategy for campaign organizations and political parties to distribute absentee ballot applications in an effort to boost the vote count for their candidates. In fact, the recent 2000 elections illustrate just how important absentee ballots really are, since several elections (the 2000 senatorial election in Washington State, for instance) were ultimately decided by absentee ballots. The final tally in California for the November 2000 elections showed that 24.5 percent of all votes were cast by absentee ballot.[6]

In 1999, California Secretary of State Bill Jones appointed a task force to investigate voting across the Internet as one way of making voting even easier. The Task Force report, released in early 2000, identified the following stages for Internet voting:

Stage One: Internet Voting from Voter's Traditional Polling Place

Stage Two: Internet Voting from any Internet Connected Polling Place

Stage Three: Remote Internet Voting from County-Controlled Computers or Kiosks

Stage Four: Remote Internet Voting from Home or Office Computers

The Task Force concluded that the first three methods were currently technologically feasible and would enhance the voting process, particularly as they would attract some of those who are least likely to vote today—those 18 to 24 years of age. However, the Task Force concluded that the last stage is the least feasible since it would produce technological threats to the security, integrity, and secrecy of the balloting process. They also determined that a comprehensive remote Internet voting system that replaced the current system was not feasible at this time due to technical and security considerations.[7]

During the 2000 elections, four California counties (Contra Costa, Sacramento, San Diego, and San Mateo) conducted a test of precinct-based Internet voting; 1,791 voters in these counties conducted a "shadow," or mock, election using Internet voting methods. Of those who voted in Contra Costa County, 100 percent found the system easy to use, although 70 percent said they had some concerns about security.[8]

THE SHRINKING
AND SHIFTING ELECTORATE

In the past three decades, we have experienced record low voter turnouts in California, with fewer than 60 percent of registered voters bothering to vote in the 1990 and 1994 gubernatorial elections. Only 62 percent of registered voters voted in the 1998 election.[9] If we consider those who were eligible to register but didn't, then less than half of those who were eligible voted. Even in presidential election years voter turnout is very low. In 1996, for example, only 29 percent of the state's eligible voters bothered to vote. In 2000, however, the final estimate of voter turnout, including all absentee ballots, was 70.9 percent, so there was considerable increase, indicating the salience of California's important position in the presidential race.[10] This declined again significantly in the November 2002 general election, when only 49.6 percent of eligible voters participated.[11]

A Slowly Shifting Electorate

California's shrinking electorate is only part of the problem. The fact that those who do vote are not representative of the larger population is disturbing. Although the gap between the voters' profile and that of the general population closed slightly in the 1998 elections, it remained far too wide in the 2000 elections.

Table 4.4 Demographic Profile of California Voters (and Unregistered Citizens)

Characteristic	All Voters	Unregistered Citizens
White	68%	39%
Latino	19	45
Black	6	4
Asian, Other	7	12
18–34	27	59
35–54	43	32
55 and older	30	9
Income under $40,000	42	65
Income $40,000 and more	58	35
Homeowner	69	37
Renter	31	63

SOURCE: Table 2-4, Public Policy Institute of California Statewide Survey, 1998, all adults. From Mark Baldassare. 2000. *California in the New Millennium: The Changing Social and Political Landscape.* Berkeley: University of California Press in conjunction with the Public Policy Institute of California, 30.

Table 4.4 indicates that the majority of those who vote are still white and middle-aged or older. The state's population, on the other hand, is becoming younger and more ethnically diverse. Simply put, there are far too many of the young and nonwhite who are turned off from politics, who feel themselves to be disenfranchised, or who just do not care about politics.

However, there are signs that voting patterns are shifting and that California still may lead the nation in the assimilation of minority groups into electoral politics. True, the number of minorities voting remains small relative to their percentage of the total population, but they are beginning to participate in larger numbers, and they are having an impact on election night. However, according to Steve Smith, "New immigrants are, by definition, noncitizens and thus nonvoters. Even those who have attained citizenship have opted out of participating in elections, some because of bad memories about politics in their homelands, others because they were still too consumed with trying to build their lives in the United States." [12]

Beginning in the 1996 elections and continuing in 1998, a greater percentage of voters were Latinos, African Americans, and Asians. The greatest increase in voter participation was in the Latino population, which promises to have a significant impact on the outcome of future elections. We have, for example, a Latino lieutenant governor and a Latino mayor of the state's third-largest city, San Jose (after Los Angeles and San Diego). Asians are also exercising their voting rights in greater numbers, although with less visible results.

Why have Latinos and Asians in particular become more active in electoral politics? Some say former Governor Pete Wilson is largely responsible because he focused his 1994 re-election campaign on Proposition 187, an initiative to cut off all but emergency services to illegal immigrants. This angered voting citizen members of these ethnic groups; he and the Republican Party further alienated these two groups when, in 1996, they supported Proposition 209, which banned affirmative action. Tony Quinn, a Republican analyst and political consultant noted, "The initiatives won, the Republicans lost." [13]

MONEY AND WINNING:
TWO FACTORS THAT GO TOGETHER

It takes money, and lots of it, to win an election in California. The 1998 elections in California were the most expensive in U.S. history. Incumbent Barbara Boxer and her challenger, Matt Fong, spent a total of $21 million in their senate race, and another $63 million was spent on the governor's race. These figures account only for the general election and do not include the millions of dollars spent in 1997 during the primary campaigns. In 2000, a less highly contested race had incumbent Senator Dianne Feinstein receiving $10,324,844, while her opponent, State Senator Tom Campbell, raised $4,659,691.[14] At the legislative level, Figure 4.1 illustrates the increasing amounts of campaign contributions that have been raised by candidates for the state assembly and senate from 1976 to 1998.

Figure 4.2 illustrates an even more important point—most of these funds have been raised by the incumbents in each of these offices, who have gone on to win most of the elections. This single point says more about politics in the state of California and in the country as a whole (where it is also true) than practically anything else. Once in office, officials tend to stay in office, and the entire campaign and campaign contribution system is oriented to keep them there.

In addition to the major statewide campaigns, hundreds of millions of dollars are spent each year on initiatives, although not all are even opposed. The 1998 Proposition 5, the "Indian gaming initiative," which allows Native Americans to have casinos on their land, cost a whopping $89 million when all costs for all sides were combined. In excess of $300 million was raised for 1998 and 2000 initiatives alone (see Table 4.5 for the amount of funds raised for and against the 2000 initiatives).

Furthermore, the financial dominance of business in political campaigns—particularly in the initiative process—is overwhelming. The Center for Government Studies, for example, found that 83 percent of the money that financed the 18 most expensive initiatives from 1956 to 1990 came from business groups.[15]

Power is the ultimate prize in the game of politics. The two best ways to measure political power are money raised and victory at the polls. Both work hand in hand—money leads to victory and victory enables the incumbent to

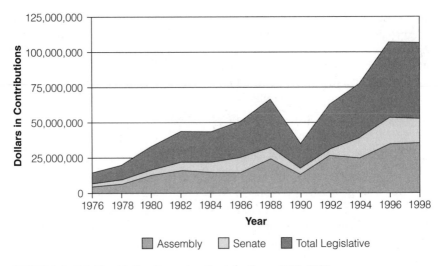

FIGURE 4.1. Total Legislative Campaign Contributions, 1976–1998

SOURCES: California Secretary of State, 2000. Analysis of Campaign Contributions. Available at
http://www.ss.ca.gov/prd/finance96/table2.htm and http://www.ss.ca.gov/prd/finance98_
general_final/figure_4.htm.

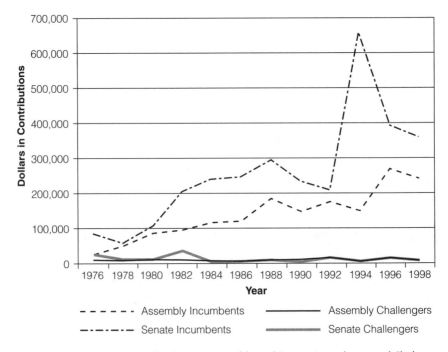

FIGURE 4.2. Campaign Contributions to Assembly and Senate Incumbents and Challengers, 1976–1998

SOURCES: California Secretary of State, 2000. Analysis of Campaign Contributions. Available at
http://www.ss.ca.gov/prd/finance98_general_final/figure_8.htm.

Table 4.5 Contributions for Year 2000 Propositions* (In Order of Most Contributions Received)

Proposition Number	Proposition Name	Dollars Received by Groups Working For Propositions	Dollars Received by Groups Working Against Propositions	Total Dollars Received
38	School Vouchers. State-Funded Private and Religious Education. Public School Funding.	$30,286,103	$29,027,509	$59,313,612
39	School Facilities. 55% Local Vote. Bonds, Taxes. Accountability Requirements.	**$27,822,935**	$2,561,082	$30,384,017
35	Public Works Projects. Use of Private Contractors for Engineering and Architectural Services.	**$11,217,656**	$8,124,813	$19,342,469
36	Drugs. Probation and Treatment Program.	**$3,691,220**	$438,507	$4,129,727
37	Fees. Vote Requirements. Taxes.	$2,427,864	**$118,919**	$2,546,783
34	Campaign Contributions and Spending. Limits. Disclosure.	**$487,472**	$637,200	$1,124,672
33	Legislature. Participation in Public Employees' Retirement System.	$92,200	**N/A**	$92,000
32	Veterans Bond Act.	**N/A**	N/A	N/A
Total	—	—	—	$116,933,280

SOURCE: Calculated from Secretary of State data, 2000. Available at http://cal-access.ss.ca.gov/contest_contrib.asp.

*Bolded totals indicate the winning side.

raise even more money for the next election. It is this fact that explains why so many Californians believe that the flood of money from special interests is at the root of the failures of the political system. Even with newly passed ethics and disclosure laws, politicians feel intense pressure to trade the long-term needs of the state for the finances that allow them to win their next election.[16]

Because money plays so important a role in election outcomes, it is all the more essential that voters pay attention to who is contributing to campaigns and how much. Today, the Internet can be a valuable resource for just this purpose. Candidates and campaigns for initiatives are required to make their

---

A Closer Look

After finding out who your state representatives are, go to http://CAL-ACCESS.ss.ca.gov to find out who gave how much money to them; for your federal representatives, go to http://www.fec.gov/finance_reports.html.

---

contribution reports public. But until recently, understanding the data was difficult. Users had to gather reams of paper and then figure out how to decipher the complicated numbers and bureaucratic jargon. While paper documents are still available from registrar offices, beginning in 1988 much of the sifting and sorting was done online by organizations and government agencies.

In the case of political campaigns, money buys access to the decision makers and in the case of initiatives, money can determine actual law. In the case of the 1998 Proposition 5 those in favor of Indian gaming outspent the opposition nearly 3 to 1 ($64 million to $25 million) and as a result they won. The influence of money in political campaigns is subtler. Assemblyman John Vasconcellos describes the process this way: "Most of us run for office because we have a certain philosophy of government we want to see embodied and developed. We don't think about economic interests. We don't realize we'll be voting between doctors and chiropractors, between psychiatrists and psychologists, between banks and savings-and-loans. So, we end up developing two roles: general government policy and arbiter between competing economic interests."[17] When they play the role of policy-maker, legislators usually act with integrity, Vasconcellos says. But when they act as arbiter, he warns, "The moral imperatives aren't as clear. In the area of psychiatrists or psychologists treating the mentally ill, unless you know the area very well, it's hard to know what's morally correct. It's thin ice, and so people are more subject to being affected by money."[18]

Clearly, an important first step in reforming the political process lies in campaign finance. If special interest influence is not curbed, there is little hope of putting the political system back on track.

THE MEDIA: INFORMATIVE
OR PROVOCATIVE?

Californians seem to be as angry with the media as they are with politicians. Television coverage of political campaigns and the policy issues of the day take the form of 15-second sound bites. Reporters often seem more interested in reporting the sensational than in helping the public to understand the implication of policy choices that would lead to informed decisions (the media's coverage of President Clinton's affair with Monica Lewinsky is only one recent and dramatic example).

Rather than appeal to the public's intellect, members of the media often manipulate public opinion with attention-getting headlines and stories on political corruption and infighting. The public must take some responsibility for this situation, however. The sensational sells newspapers and TV news programs. If members of the public were interested in in-depth, balanced reporting on the issues, they would watch substantive news shows such as *Meet the Press* and public television news programming.

It has become an axiom in American politics that a certain tension and wariness exists in the dealings between reporters and politicians. That is certainly the case in California. Gone are the days when most of the Capitol press corps and the state's political media were part of the inside establishment. Gone are the times when most reporters and politicians ate, drank, and caroused together, and neither group judged the other too harshly. What has emerged instead is constant sparring and occasional slugging between politicians and news people, two groups who need each other and, frankly, hate it.[19]

California's size and the fact that it is the center for much of the nation's radio, television, and film industry makes it a media state. Candidates are very dependent on the mass media to get their message to the public since the state is a thousand miles in length and made up of many different constituencies to persuade. Unfortunately, in recent years the media have devoted less time to state and local politics—particularly the day-to-day coverage of political decision-making—except at election time.

We live in the age of "spin doctors." Putting the best face on things and influencing public opinion seem more important than ever. For this reason, political public relation firms are vitally important to both politicians and to those who want to influence politicians. In fact, political PR firms have become as important as lobbyists in influence peddling. Laureen Lazarovici writes, "If you view politicians as people who lick their fingers and hold them to the wind, political public relations practitioners are the windmakers."[20]

In the old days, interest groups would hire a lobbyist to pressure the legislature to act on their behalf. This process is no longer sufficient to get what interest groups want in Sacramento. Now, interest groups sometimes find it more effective to get their message across to the public first and, in turn, have the public pressure their state legislators. "Increasingly, lobbyists are bringing us on board on the front end," says Donna Lucas, president of Nelson & Lucas Communications and former deputy press secretary to ex-Governor George Deukmejian.[21]

Why are public relations firms so influential today? One reason is the increased ubiquity of technology, including databases, cell phones, pagers, instant messaging, and the Internet, which all work to speed communication. It isn't the only reason, however. Term limits are given most of the credit by those in the PR business. Term limits have created much more turnover among officeholders so lasting coalitions and the ability to organize at the grassroots level are critical. Officeholders need to know what is happening with their constituents, and public relations professionals can make those views known.

In the past, the success of lobbyists had been in their ability to form long-term relationships with legislators. Lobbyists depended on whom they knew even more than on what they knew. Term limits changed the nature of the game. Because legislators are limited to no more than six years in the assembly and eight years in the senate, lobbyists must access officeholders' constituents rather than just develop and then appeal to relationships. The use of public relations firms is even more critical in waging a successful initiative campaign.

Political public relations firms learned from the successes of various grassroots organizations in the 1980s. As Lazarovici states, "It's ironic that 'grassroots'—once the buzzword for populist causes like environmentalism, union organizing and consumer rights—is now becoming the domain of button-down public relations professionals representing large corporate interests."[22]

Public relations firms may want to be seen as part of the grassroots political scene and not be lumped into the same category as lobbyists; the fact remains that they are highly paid professionals who are in the business of influencing public opinion on behalf of special interest groups. They are hardly naive, innocent, underpaid people working for the underdog, as they would have people believe.

ELECTIONS, MEDIA, MONEY, AND THE INTERNET

The widespread usage of the Internet has spurred the already intense relationships between the electoral process, the media, and money. Given the size of the California media market and the important role and wide presence of the Internet throughout the state, California politics promises to be a bellwether for how these interactions will play out on the national scene. Scholars of California politics can now only guess at the ultimate impacts of these important processes. The next few years will be critical ones in determining how the effects of the media, the Internet, money, and factors like term limits will affect the electorate, officeholders, public policy, and politics itself.

ADDITIONAL RESOURCES

Broder, David S. 2000. *Democracy Derailed: Initiative Campaigns and the Power of Money.* New York: James H. Silberman Book—Harcourt Inc.

California Secretary of State Campaign Finance Information. Available at http://www.ss.ca.gov/prd/prd.htm.

Keith, Bruce E. *The Myth of the Independent Voter.* Berkeley: University of California Press, 1992.

Owens, R. John. Costantini, Edmund, and Weschler, Louis F. *California Politics and Parties.* New York: Macmillan, 1970.

A Closer Look

What do you think will happen to California elections—the role of the media, and the need for money to run campaigns—now that the Internet and the World Wide Web have become ever-present in our lives?

NOTES

1. Jill Lawrence, *USA Today,* March 26, 1999, 1.

2. League of Women Voters, *Guide to California Government,* 14th ed. (Sacramento, CA: League of Women Voters Education Fund, 1992), 14.

3. California Secretary of State. 2001. Procedure for Recall of State and Local Officials Secretary of State's Office. Available at http://www.ss.ca.gov/elections/recall.pdf.

4. To recall a statewide officeholder, signatures equivalent to 12 percent of the most recent vote for that office and signatures from at least five counties equal to 1 percent of the last vote for that office in that county are required. A petition to recall a state legislator, judge, or member of the Board of Equalization must have signatures equal to 20 percent of the last vote for the office. Recall proponents have 160 days in which to file the signed petition.

5. League of Women Voters, 7.

6. California Secretary of State, 2000. Jones Officially Certifies California Election Results. Available at http://www.ss.ca.gov/executive/press_releases/2000/00-131.htm, December 15, 2000.

7. California Internet Voting Task Force, 2000. Final Report Online. Available at California Secretary of State, http://www.ss.ca.gov/executive/ivote.

8. California Secretary of State. 2000. Online Voting Demonstrations. Available at http://www.ss.ca.gov/elections/elections_online_demo.htm.

9. *San Francisco Chronicle,* November 4, 1998, A18.

10. California Secretary of State, 2000. Jones Officially Certifies California Election Results. Available at http://www.ss.ca.gov/executive/press_releases/2000/00-131.htm, December 15, 2000.

11. California Secretary of State. 2002. County Status in Voter 2002. Office of Secretary of State. Available at http://vote2002.ss.ca.gov/Returns/status.htm.

12. Steve Scott, "Reality Votes: California's Political Demographics Are Slowly Growing More in Sync with Its Overall Demographics. How Will This Change Affect the Way Elections Are Run—and Won—in 1998 and Beyond?" *California Government & Politics Annual,* 55.

13. Ibid., 55.

14. U.S. Federal Election Commission. 2000. Campaign Finance Reports and Data. Available at http://www.fec.gov/finance_reports.html.

15. *San Francisco Chronicle,* May 19, 1998, A19.

16. Charles Lacy et al., "Politics in California: How Can We Make the System Work?" California Issues Forums, University Extension, University of California, Davis, 1993, 13.

17. A. G. Block, "The Ethics Jungle: Making Moral Judgments in a Practical World," *California Journal,* April 1990, 176.

18. Ibid., 176.

19. Dan Walters, "Press vs. Politicians— Never-Ending War," *California Government & Politics Annual 1995–1996* (Sacramento, CA: Journal Press, 1995), 477.

20. Laureen Lazarovici, "The Rise of the Wind-Makers: Political Public Relations Firms Grow More Powerful," *California Journal,* June 1995, 16.

21. Ibid., 16.

22. Ibid., 19.

5

Paying for What California Cares About: Budget Receipts and Expenditures

In 1998, Californians passed Proposition 10, a measure to add $0.50 surtax per pack of cigarettes and an even higher surtax on other tobacco products. Like many other fiscal measures, this proposition had two related goals—to raise money (and perhaps reduce demand for cigarettes) and to influence some social goal (in this case, programs for children's health and development). This proposition set off a cavalcade of court challenges and Proposition 28, an initiative on the March 7, 2000, ballot. Proposition 28 was an unsuccessful effort to repeal Proposition 10. Both of these measures are examples of the political nature of the financial process and how it can be used for social purposes.

The true values of any jurisdiction or government can be found in their budgets—the funds they receive and how those funds are spent. This chapter describes the sources and uses of California's public monies at both the state and county levels—how the government pays for what Californians care about. This chapter also discusses the state budget process, Proposition 13, and its impact on public revenue generation and expenditure.

CALIFORNIA'S MONEY

Almost all of California's income revenue is placed into one fund called the General Fund. This important fund is the predominant one for financing state government programs. The primary sources of revenue for the General Fund

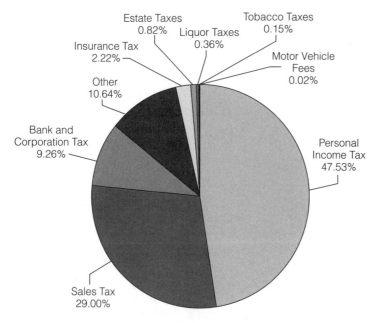

FIGURE 5.1. California Revenues, 2002–2003

SOURCE: California Department of Finance, 2002. California State Budget Highlights 2002–2003.
Available at http://www.dof.ca.gov/HTML/BUD_DOCS/State_Budget_Highlights.pdf.

are the personal income tax, sales tax, and bank and corporation taxes. The General Fund is used as the major funding source for all levels of education, health and welfare programs, youth and adult correctional programs, and tax relief.[1]

Other important funds include Special Funds, where monies for special purposes are placed, and Bond Funds, where money raised to build large projects tends to reside. Special Funds is a generic term used for "governmental cost funds" other than the General Fund. Governmental cost funds are commonly defined as those funds used to account for revenues from taxes, licenses, and fees where the use of such revenues is restricted by law for particular functions or activities of government (e.g., fish and game, regulation of professions).[2]

Sources of State Revenue

Most of the revenue brought into the state government comes from taxes. The remainder comes from fees and from intergovernmental transfers, such as grant monies from the federal government. The tax system is elaborate; it supports most state-funded, and many local units of government-funded, programs. For each fiscal year (beginning each July 1 and continuing until the next June 30), total sources of General Fund monies are generally broken down into ten separate categories (see Figure 5.1). For 2002–2003, personal income (47.5 percent of total) and sales taxes (29 percent) are by far the most important, comprising

76.5 percent of all General Fund revenues. Bank and corporation taxes comprise only 9.3 percent, whereas other sources together comprise only 14 percent
of total revenues.[3]

Between 1998 and 2001, California revenues exceeded expectations. When
the economy grows, individuals and corporations make more money; therefore, the taxes due to the federal and state governments also increase. However,
personal income taxes for 2001–2002 and 2002–2003 were down significantly
from 2000–2001, when they comprised 55 percent of total revenues. This decline is attributed to the collapse of the dot-com industry and the recession felt
throughout California and the entire country, which caused this decline in personal income taxes on capital gains and stock options. The revised 2002–2003
Governor's General Fund budget was based upon revenues of $79,158 billion
for a total budget of $98,888 billion (this includes the General Fund, Special
Funds, and Bond Funds).[4]

Where the Money Goes

When there is a surplus, the discussion between policy-makers turns to how to
spend the extra funds, and that discussion dominated the 2000–2001 legislative session (at least until the California energy crisis hit in 2000). In 2002–
2003, the discussion is quite different, and the quick turnaround was quite difficult for many to absorb as cuts were discussed and decisions were made. The
2002–2003 final budget (see Figure 5.2) passed by the legislature and approved
by the governor showed a distribution of expenditures with K–12 education
receiving the most funds (40.1 percent), and Environmental Protection/Con-
sumer Services and Business/Transportation/Housing tying the other for receiving the least (0.2 percent).[5]

Figure 5.3 shows how the distribution of expenditures has changed over
time. K–12 education has maintained its position as the top priority of California policy-makers while health and human services has slowly declined
from 33 percent in 1980–81 to 26 percent in 2000–2001. Higher education
has gained slightly (up four percentage points to 17 percent) and corrections
peaked at 9 percent in 1994–1995, then slightly declined to 7 percent in 2000–
2001.[6]

Some of these policies changed in 2001, when policy-makers debated how
to spend the unexpected funds from the then-surplus. According to the California Budget Project, the real winners of the debate over how to spend the unexpected funds were Business, Transportation, and Housing (620 percent increase

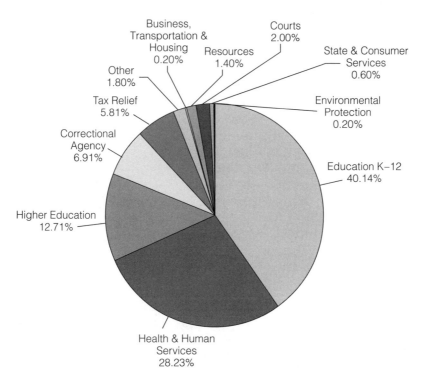

FIGURE 5.2. California Budgeted General Fund Expenditures, 2002–2003

SOURCE: California Department of Finance, 2002. California State Budget Highlights 2002–2003. Available at http://www.dof.ca.gov/HTML/BUD_DOCS/State_Budget_Highlights.pdf.

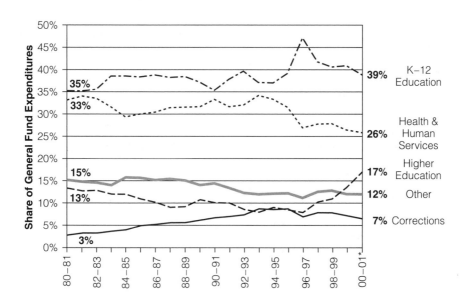

FIGURE 5.3. Spending as Proportion of Total General Fund Spending

SOURCE: California Budget Project. 2000. K–12 Education Continues to Absorb Largest Share of State General Fund Spending. File cbp0007.xls. Available at http://www.cbp.org.

in spending) and General Government (160 percent increase). Most of the funds in the Business, Transportation, and Housing category went to Governor Davis's Traffic Congestion Relief Plan ($1.5 billion) and to housing. In the General Government category, most of the change was attributed to funds sent to cities and counties to help them deal with a loss of funds from the Vehicle License Fee tax rate reduction to citizens. Some of the extra money also went to Corrections for employee compensation, to higher education (for enrollment increases, summer class fee reductions, and employee compensation), and to K–12 education (for teacher recruitment and retention and inflation adjustments).[7] This surplus has now totally disappeared, used up by the energy crisis, the slowing economy, and the loss of the dot.com industry plus the decline of the stock market.

The Deficit

This debate shifted totally in 2002–2003, when, for only the third time in 50 years, the state budget showed a decline in overall expenditure levels, attributed to the deficit caused by the deficit, the dot-com collapse, and the recession.[8] These events led to an expected cumulative deficit anywhere from $26.1 billion to $34.6 billion in 2003–2004, including a shortfall of $6.1 billion in the 2002–2003 budget year. Beyond 2003–2004, the state legislative analyst is forecasting $12 billion to $16 billion deficits per year unless action is taken.[9] As stated earlier, much of this deficit is due to the recession and a decline in revenues from personal income taxes—to be specific, from declines in investment-related income from capital gains and stock options.

Conflicts will continue and deepen over how to resolve these deficits, in other words, over whether to further increase revenues or to make additional cuts in spending. As one sign of the difficulties of the decisions that need to be made, the state assembly and senate took longer in 2002 to pass the state budget than any other year, including the 1992–1993 session, a time of extreme budgetary deficits.[10]

Forty other states were experiencing deficits in 2002 and 2003, as well, and many of them also experienced their deficits as a sudden turnaround.

THE STATE BUDGET PROCESS

A state budget is the single most sweeping piece of state legislation in any year. It defines the governor's and legislature's priorities on everything from schools and colleges to flood control projects, health care, prisons, and parks.[11] The budget is the result of a process that begins more than one year before the budget becomes law:

1. Governor's priorities start the process. The process begins when the Department of Finance informs various state agencies of the governor's priorities for the next year.

2. Based upon that guidance, departments prepare their budget requests. Each department then prepares recommendations that fit the governor's priorities in two ways: program and policy changes in part one and anticipated demand for goods and services in part two. This part is often called "enrollment, caseload, and population changes." Enrollment applies to education, caseload to health and welfare, and population to corrections.

3. Department of Finance prepares final governor's budget. This information is forwarded to the Department of Finance, which advises the governor in making budget decisions. The governor prepares the budget according to his own priorities and based upon the recommendations of the departments.

4. Governor's budget goes to the legislature for approval. That budget is presented to the legislature on January 10 of each year. At that time, it incorporates revenue and expenditure estimates based on information available through late December of the previous year. The budget, now referred to as the budget bill, must be passed by June 15. The state's fiscal year runs July 1 to June 30. Should the governor want to change the budget presented to the legislature (including adjustments resulting from changes in population or demands for goods or services), the Department of Finance proposes adjustments in the Governor's Budget to the legislature during budget hearings and through Finance Letters, formal statements of recommendations.

5. May Revision of budget goes to legislature. In the late spring, usually May and June, the Department of Finance submits revised expenditure and revenue estimates for both the current and budget (next) years to the legislature. This update process is referred to as the May Revision and the product itself as the May Revise. The Department of Finance also prepares monthly economic and cash revenue updates during the fiscal year.

6. Legislature reviews and analyses budget. During the legislature's review and actions on the budget bill, both houses are advised primarily by the Legislative Analyst's Office (LAO). Concomitantly, the staffs of both the Assembly Ways and Means Committee and the Senate Budget and Fiscal Review Committee, and their respective subcommittees, review the bill.[12] The primary activity of the LAO is to review both the expenditure levels and the revenue projections of the governor's office. Frequently there is a difference of opinion as to the accuracy of the revenue projections and recommended changes to the governor's budget. In addition, the LAO analysis does not always agree with that of the Department of Finance, particularly as the Department of Finance is an executive branch administrative function under the governor, while the LAO operates under the auspices of the legislative branch of state government.[13]

7. Legislature approves the budget. Once discussion of the bill goes to the floor of either house, a two-thirds vote is required to approve the budget.

The two-thirds vote requirement is an unusually stringent level of consensus. Many efforts to reform the budget process argue that a simple majority vote would streamline the process. An identical budget bill must pass both houses by this two-thirds vote. Since this seldom happens, a conference committee, composed of members from each house, is formed to forge a compromise. The conference committee issues a report that goes back to both houses to be voted upon as is. The report cannot be amended on the floor of either chamber.

8. Governor must approve final version of legislative budget. When an identical bill finally passes both houses by a two-thirds vote, it is sent to the governor for action. The governor has 12 working days to act on the budget bill. The governor can eliminate or reduce certain measures through a line-item veto. However, the governor cannot add or increase appropriations at this point. Once the governor makes final decisions on line-item vetoes, the budget bill is signed and goes into effect on July 1. The final budget is referred to as the "final change book."

9. Budget takes effect and the process begins again. By the time the budget takes effect, this process is already under way for the following fiscal year.

Table 5.1 itemizes the key actors, purposes, document titles, and time frames used in the budget process.

California's budget process is incremental in nature. This means that the previous year's budget is a baseline or starting point for the next year's budget. Adjustments are made that reflect increases in costs and increased demand for a program or service. Public policy decisions regarding whether programs or services should continue or be drastically changed are rarely addressed.

California uses a combination program/line-item budget process and format that combines information about programs with information about individual types of expenditures, or line items. The incremental process and line-item/program budgeting are compatible. However, they have their shortcomings.

An incremental budgeting process seldom provides an overall picture of a program or service. It provides little information about program impact or effectiveness of service delivery. It never questions the continued legitimacy of the program or service. Line-item budgeting is primarily an accounting tool, not a policy-setting tool, and reflects the status quo unless a concerted political effort is made to change public policy. Combining line items with information about overall programs is an attempt to overcome those shortcomings.

The Legislative Analyst's Office (LAO) reviews the budget each year on behalf of the legislature and makes its recommendations and analysis. The LAO also provides analysis of the state department's implementation of the approved budget. However, LAO review of program effectiveness tends to get lost in the incremental and line-item nature of the state budget process, even with the use of program budgetary organization.

Table 5.1 California Budget Process

Title	Purpose	Prepared/Issued By	When
Budget Letters/ Memos	Provide administration/ Guidelines to agencies and departments	Governor/Department of Finance	January– December
Budget Change Proposal	Document what to maintain/change in existing service levels	Agencies/departments submit to Department of Finance	July– September
Governor's Budget	Proposed budget for the governor/Next fiscal year	Department of Finance	January 10
Governor's Budget Summary	A summary of the budget	Governor/Department of Finance	January 10
Budget Bill	Legislative decision document/ authorization for governor's expenditure plans	Department of Finance/ Legislature	January 10
Budget Analysis	Analysis of budget bill	LAO	February
May Revision	Update General Fund revenues/expenses/ reserves	Department of Finance	Mid–May
Budget Act	Passed by the legislature/Signed by the governor	Legislature/Governor	Late June
Final Budget Summary	Update individual items, including governor's vetoes	Department of Finance	Late July
Final Change Book	Update details in the Governor's Budget	Department of Finance	Late July

SOURCE: Governor's Budget Summary, 1999–2000, Appendix 1.

Even more complicated than the involved legislative, executive, and bureaucracy-based process is the reality of the involvement of citizen-initiated propositions in the state and local budgeting process. Fiscal decision-making is a complicated process, with many interlocking factors impacting the process. The passage of some propositions can have contradictory effects, can lock the state into fiscal decisions that can impact other areas of the budget, and in general strictly limits the flexibility of fiscal decision-makers. Many propositions have had enormous impacts upon the state's fiscal and general policy context—the most important of which is undoubtedly Proposition 13 in 1978, which limited property tax rates. As Table 5.2 indicates, the California Legislative Analyst's Office suggests that 14 different propositions have had major state and local fiscal impacts since 1978.[14]

Table 5.2 Initiative Measures That Have Had Major State-Local Fiscal Implications

Proposition (Election)	Major Provisions
13 (June 1978)	Limits general property tax rates to 1 percent. Limits increases in assessed value after a property is bought or constructed. Makes legislature responsible for dividing property tax among local entities. Requires two-thirds vote for legislature to increase taxes, and two-thirds voter approval of new local special taxes.
4 (November 1979)	Generally limits spending by the state and local entities to prior-year amount, adjusted for population growth and inflation (per capita personal income growth). Requires state to reimburse local entities for mandated costs.
6 (June 1982)	Prohibits state gift and inheritance taxes except for "pickup" tax qualifying for federal tax credit.
7 (June 1982)	Requires indexing of state personal income tax brackets for inflation.
37 (November 1984)	Establishes state lottery and dedicates a portion of revenue to education. Places prohibition of casino gambling in state constitution.
62 (November 1986)	Requires approval of new local general taxes by two-thirds of the governing body and a majority of local voters (excludes charter cities).
98 (November 1988)	Establishes minimum state funding guarantee for K–12 schools and community colleges.
99 (November 1988)	Imposes a $.25 per pack surtax on cigarettes and a comparable surtax on other tobacco products. Limits use of surtax revenue, primarily to augment health-related programs.
162 (November 1992)	Limits the legislature's authority over Public Employee Retirement System (PERS) and other public retirement systems, including their administrative costs and actuarial assumptions.
163 (November 1992)	Repealed "snack tax" and prohibits any future sales tax on food items, including candy, snacks, and bottled water.
172 (November 1992)	Imposes half-cent sales tax and dedicates the revenue to local public safety programs.
218 (November 1996)	Limits authority of local governments to impose taxes and property-related assessments, fees, and charges. Requires majority of voters to approve increases in all general taxes, and reiterates that two-thirds must approve special taxes.
10 (November 1998)	Imposes a $.50 per pack surtax on cigarettes, and higher surtax on other tobacco products. Limits use of revenues, primarily to augment early childhood development programs.
39 (November 2000)	Allows 55 percent of voters to approve local general obligation bonds for school facilities.

SOURCE: Legislative Analyst's Office. 2000. CAL Facts: California's Economy and Budget in Perspective. Available at http://www.lao.ca.gov/2000_reports/calfacts/2000_calfacts_pdf_toc.html, 27–28, December 2000.

PROPOSITION 13

California's economy in the 1970s resulted in large state government surpluses. The state had a $3.6 billion surplus in the 1977–1978 fiscal year.[15] In the June 1978 primary, the Jarvis-Gann initiative, Proposition 13, passed with 65 percent of the vote.[16] Proposition 13 reflected public anger at escalating property taxes in an era of state budget surpluses. This proposition had little impact on the financing of statewide programs, since the state government does not rely on local property tax to pay for what it spends. However, the property tax prior to Proposition 13 was a major source of income for school districts, cities, counties, and single-purpose special districts (e.g., a library district).

Proposition 13 made six changes to the state constitution:[17]

Property tax rates were capped at 1 percent of full cash value at the time of acquisition.

Property values for tax purposes were rolled back to their 1975–1976 level.

Responsibility for allocating property tax revenues among local jurisdictions was transferred to state lawmakers.

It replaced the annual reassessment of property at full cash value with a system based on cost at acquisition. Property is assessed at market value for tax purposes only when it changes ownership. Increases in the value are limited to an annual inflation factor of no more than 2 percent.

Any legislation increasing state revenues must be approved by a two-thirds vote of each house of the legislature.

Taxes raised by local units of government for a designated or "special" purpose must be approved by two-thirds of the voters.

The state legislature, under Senate Bill 154 and Assembly Bill 8, originally chose to "bail out" local governments by providing them with a share of the state general fund surplus. This allowed the state to comply with the court-imposed provisions of *Serrano v. Priest*. In this case (1971), the California State Supreme Court ruled that per-pupil spending must be equal across the state's numerous school districts; the ruling was a major contributor to the state's decline in national ranking on per-pupil expenditures, from eleventh in 1970 to thirtieth 20 years later.[18]

While the initiative allowed increases in property taxes, it did not mandate the apportionment of the remaining property taxes. This uncertain situation resulted in many years of litigation, exacerbated by the severe state recession during the 1980s and early 1990s. It also brought about shifts in property tax from cities and counties back to schools early in the 1990s.

As a result of the constraints imposed by Proposition 13, cities have increasingly turned to fees and increased sales taxes for financing local government services, which had previously been financed by either the state general fund or local property taxes.[19]

CITY AND COUNTY FINANCES

City and county finances are based upon a quite different set of revenues and expenditure responsibilities. As in other years, most 1999–2000 county revenues came from other levels of government (20 percent federal, 33.7 percent state), from property taxes (10.5 percent), from fees for various services (22.5 percent), and from charges for Enterprise activities like airports, hospitals, refuse, and transportation (13 percent).[20]

California cities in 1998–1999, on the other hand, only received 6.4 percent from their property taxes, another 9.7 percent from sales and use taxes, and another 14.6 percent from other taxes. They are also much more dependent upon service fees than are counties (39.7 percent). However, this figure is artificially inflated since it includes those cities that own their own electric utility and so, receive electric fees directly from consumers. Cities are also less dependent than counties upon the state and the federal government—they receive only 12.8 percent of their total revenues from those sources.[21]

Due to their particular sources of revenues, cities and counties are subject to more economic shifts than are other levels of government. In addition, when the state or federal governments have to cut their own budgets, cities and counties receive less from them and so their own budgets are also reduced. This is even more problematic in 2003, when the state is considering reducing its deficit by "realigning" services, transferring them to country governments.

The types of expenditures and service responsibilities that exist for counties and cities are also different from those of the state and federal government. For counties, the largest expenditure categories are public assistance programs (34.3 percent of total expenditures), public protection (police and fire protection, 30 percent), health and sanitation (17.3 percent), and general expenditures (9.9 percent).[22]

Cities spend their money on much of the same types of categories, with public protection a very high priority. In 1998–1999, most expenditures were spent on public protection (26.6 percent of their total expenditures), community development and health (20.9 percent), public utilities (19.5 percent), and transportation (14.8 percent). Education is also an important local function but in California, revenues (property taxes) and expenditures for schools are in the hands of school districts, not directly under counties or cities.[23]

IMPACT OF INTERNET-BASED E-COMMERCE ACTIVITIES

One new and very important emerging issue that is already having an enormous impact upon California's state and local finances is that of Internet taxation. Currently, when consumers purchase goods in a traditional store, they pay sales taxes to the business, which passes them on to the state and local government. If consumers purchase an item from a catalog over the telephone, they typically pay sales taxes on that item.

A Closer Look

Read the property tax bill of someone that you know. What is included on the bill? In addition to paying to support your local county, are there school districts on the bill? Special districts? How much does each of these districts get in property taxes from you or your friend? How much do you know about the work that each of these jurisdictions does with this money?

However, if consumers purchase an item from an Internet e-commerce Web site, they do not pay sales or any other taxes on that item (from practically all states). During the third quarter of 2002, the U.S. Census Bureau estimated e-commerce activity at $11.1 billion, an increase of 34.4 percent from the third quarter 2001 estimates.[24] So this economic activity is quite significant, and the amount of taxes that state and local governments, the primary recipient of sales taxes, are losing is also quite significant.

Due to the sheer numbers of high technology and e-commerce firms (dot.com companies) and activity in the state, California stands to lose more than most jurisdictions. The Congressional Internet Caucus Committee estimates that if businesses are not soon required to collect and pass on use or sales taxes, by the year 2003 California will have lost $2.29 billion in revenue. This is 11.4 percent of the total revenue estimated to be lost across the entire country—$20.1 billion.[25]

The issue is very divisive with strong supporters on either side. On one side are state and local governments concerned about losing the revenue. On the other side are businesses and federal officials, concerned that the growing Internet e-commerce activity will lose its momentum and slow down. In 1998, the Internet Tax Freedom Act was passed, putting a three-year moratorium upon taxing Internet access and goods purchased on the Internet. It also created an advisory committee to study the issue. In 2001, the Act was extended for an additional two years so discussion and debate on this important issue continues. Some have proposed a plan to have a national sales tax on e-commerce purchases, with the funds to then be distributed to the appropriate state and local jurisdictions, while others want no taxation on digital products. To date, this issue is still unresolved.

BUDGETING IN THE FUTURE

The state as well as our cities and counties will have fiscal difficulties as long as the citizenry of California expect their government to do more with less. Insistence on lower taxes is incompatible with initiatives that earmark and restrict the use of funds for certain areas (such as Proposition 182 regarding schools) as well as the tough-on-crime laws such as the "Three Strikes and You're Out."

A Closer Look

In general, should taxes be raised or expenditures decreased in order to reduce deficits? If expenditures should be cut, which expenditure areas should be reduced? What state or local services do *you* think you can do without?

Why? Which taxes are appropriate to increase—why or why not?

Yet, because the stakes are so high, the conflict and debates are so intense—and difficult to resolve. Californians' desire to spend more without a recognition of the availability of tax revenues to finance programs or services is both inconsistent and, ultimately, not sustainable.

ADDITIONAL RESOURCES

California Budget Project Web site. Available at http://www.cbp.org.

California Department of Finance Web site. Available at http://www.dof.ca.gov.

California Budget Documents Web site. Available at http://www.dof.ca .gov/HTML/BUD_DOCS/Bud_ link.htm.

Reid, Gary J. "How Cities in California Responded to Fiscal Pressures Since Proposition 13," *Public Budgeting and Finance*, 8:1 (1988).

NOTES

1. California Department of Finance. 2000. Governor's Budget Summary, Appendix 6.

2. Ibid.

3. California Department of Finance, 2002. California State Budget Highlights 2002–2003. Available at http://www.dof .ca.gov/HTML/BUD_DOCS/State_ Budget_Highlights.pdf.

4. Ibid.

5. Ibid.

6. California Budget Project. 2000. K–12 Education Continues to Absorb Largest Share of State General Fund Spending. File cbp0007.xls. Available at http://www .cbp.org.

7. California Budget Project. 2000. *Budget Watch* 6 (3): October 2000, 1–3.

8. California Department of Finance, 2002. California State Budget Highlights 2002–2003. Available at http://www.dof .ca.gov/HTML/BUD_DOCS/State_ Budget_Highlights.pdf.

9. Legislative Analyst's Office. 2002. California's Fiscal Outlook: LAO Projections, 2002–03 through 2007–08. Sacramento. Available at http://www.lao.ca.gov/2002/ fiscal_outlook/fiscal_outlook_2002.html. California Budget Project. 2003. Bridging the Gap: The Social and Economic Context of the Governor's Proposed 2003-2004 Budget. Available at www .cbp.org

10. California Budget Project. 2002. Budget Passed after Record Delay. Available at http://www.cbp.org/2002/bwvol83.htm.

11. *Los Angeles Times,* January 9, 1999, A1.

12. Richard Krolak, *California's Budget Dance: Issues and Process,* Sacramento: California Journal Press, 1990, 77.

13. Students can research the differences in the analysis of both the Department of Finance and the LAO by checking their Web sites as follows: State Department of Finance: http://www.dof.ca.gov; the LAO: http://www.lao.gov.

14. Legislative Analyst's Office. 2000. CAL Facts: California's Economy and Budget in Perspective. Available at http://www.lao.ca.gov/2000_reports/calfacts/2000_calfacts_pdf_toc.html, 27–28, December 2000.

15. Bernard L. Hynk, Seymon Brown, and Ernest W. Thacker, *Politics and Government in California,* 10th ed., Harper & Row, 1979, 213.

16. *San Francisco Chronicle,* May 20, 1998, A10.

17. California Voter Project, *San Francisco Chronicle,* May 20, 1998, A10.

18. Fabio Silva and Jon Sonstelie, "Did *Serrano* Cause a Decline in School Spending?" *National Tax Journal,* v. 2 n. 2, 199–215.

19. Statement of Vote, Secretary of State, 1998.

20. California State Controller's Office. 2002. State of California Counties Annual Report (Fiscal Year 1999–2000) Sacramento: California State Controller's Office, iii. Available at http://www.sco.ca.gov/ard/local/locrep/counties/9900/counties9900.pdf.

21. California State Controller's Office. 2002. State of California Cities Annual Report (Fiscal Year 1998–1999) Sacramento: California State Controller's Office, iii. Available at http://www.sco.ca.gov/ard/local/locrep/cities/9899/9899citiespub.pdf.

22. California State Controller's Office. 2002. State of California Counties Annual Report (Fiscal Year 1999–2000) Sacramento: California State Controller's Office, xii. Available at http://www.sco.ca.gov/ard/local/locrep/counties/9900/counties9900.pdf.

23. California State Controller's Office. 2002. State of California Cities Annual Report (Fiscal Year 1998–1999). Sacramento: California State Controller's Office, iii. Available at http://www.sco.ca.gov/ard/local/locrep/cities/9899/9899citiespub.pdf.

24. U.S. Census Bureau. 2002. U.S. Department of Commerce News. Available at http://www.census.gov/mrts/www/current.html.

25. Advisory Committee, Congressional Internet Caucus. 2000. Internet Taxation Compilation Book. Available at http://www.netcaucus.org/books/taxation.

6

The Executive Branch

In some form or other nearly every governmental problem that involves the health, the happiness, or the prosperity of the State has arisen, because some private interest has intervened or has sought for its own gain to exploit either the resources or the politics of the State. I take it, therefore, that the first duty that is mine to perform is to eliminate every private interest from the government, and to make the public service of the State responsive solely to the people.

HIRAM JOHNSON, GOVERNOR, 1911–1917

Their solution [referring to his opponents] cannot be found in narrow partisanship any more than world problems can be solved through extreme nationalism. They only can be solved through independent, humane, forward-looking and financially sound government. . . . Happiness is best advanced where there is the greatest spirit of harmony, where opportunity in life is equal, where there is no squalor, where the health of people is protected, and where the dignity of the human personality is recognized without regard to race or creed. None of these things follow from mere numbers. They must be sought after, planned for and perfected as built-in segments of our social structure. I would urge every university, college, school, church, business and labor group, indeed every family to face squarely to the fact that we have the problem of providing for the happiness of more people than any state in the Union. And I would emphasize the fact that the millions to whose happiness we are dedicating ourselves are our children and their children. What better heritage could we leave them.

EARL WARREN, GOVERNOR, 1943–1953

My son asked me what I hoped to accomplish as governor. I told him, essentially, to make life more comfortable for people, as far as government can. I think that embraces everything from developing the water resources vital to California's growth, to getting a man to work and back fifteen minutes earlier if it can be done through a state highway program.

EDMOND G. "PAT" BROWN SR., GOVERNOR, 1959–1967

I don't believe in government that protects us from ourselves. Government is not the solution to our problem; government is the problem. From time to time we've been tempted to believe that society has become too complex to be managed by self-rule, that government by an elite group is superior to government for, by, and of the people. But if no one among us is capable of governing ourselves, then who among us has the capacity to govern someone else? All of us together—in and out of government—must bear the burden. The solutions we seek must be equitable with no one group singled out to pay a higher price.

RONALD REAGAN, GOVERNOR, 1967–1975

We live in an era of limits. . . . Small is beautiful. . . . If we stop building things, people won't come. . . . As a small minority of the world's population, we cannot sustain a way of life that uses one-third of the world's basic resources for but a few percent of its people, but we can invent new ways to live better. We can learn to place quality above quantity and caring above consumption.

JERRY BROWN, GOVERNOR, 1975–1983

The question isn't whether California will change but how it will change. I'm convinced it not only doesn't have to deteriorate, but it can have a brilliant future. . . . The Governor of California must be many things—a crisis manager when the earth shakes or the forest burns, a booster for California jobs across the country and around the world, a person of conviction who will stand up for what's right no matter what the consequences or who's opposed. But today, above all, the Governor of California must be one thing—a leader, a leader who can bring California through these times to a future of new hope and opportunity.

PETE WILSON, GOVERNOR, 1991–1999

Today we begin a new chapter in the history of California: The Era of
Higher Expectations. We will embark in a new direction guided by our
lasting values. . . . Californians are essentially moderate, pragmatic people,
more interested in practical solutions to their problems than in rigid
ideologies. I am a moderate and a pragmatist by nature. . . . That is how I
will lead this state into the future. I will govern neither from the right nor
from the left, but from the center, propelled not by ideology, but by
common sense that seeks better results for all of us. . . . I pledged that the day
I took the oath of office, the era of wedge-issue politics in California would
be over. Well, my fellow Californians, that day is here. That time is now. And
you can finally ring down the curtain on the politics of division. . . . We are
America's future. This great, bold experiment on the Pacific is America's
future. And we can either allow society to be torn by factions and disunity,
or we can demonstrate to the world how a heterogeneous people can live and
prosper together. Our vast diversity is our strength.

GRAY DAVIS, GOVERNOR, 1999–PRESENT

E very governor brings to the office a different view of the role of government
in society that is, in large measure, a reflection of the times in which he lives.
The quote from Governor Johnson, for example, reflects his desire (and that of
the Progressives) to rid government of undue influence by the powerful interests of the railroads and industrialists. He believed that government was to serve
the people and not special interest groups.

Earl Warren and Edmond "Pat" Brown also felt strongly that government
should be instrumental in providing for the health and happiness of all people,
regardless of race or social class. They governed during times of economic
prosperity and growth in California, and both used the opportunity to build an
infrastructure—schools, roads, dams, and aqueducts—in California that was
unparalleled in the country.

Ronald Reagan, on the other hand, believed that government was as much
the problem as the solution to the social and economic ills that plagued society. He placed far more faith in the private sector to provide for the health and
well-being of citizens than did his predecessors, Johnson, Warren, and Brown
Sr. His philosophy held that people needed to be more self-reliant and not turn
to government for assistance. The primary role of government was to protect
against aggressors (e.g., military and police functions) and to provide for our
general safety (e.g., fire). His philosophy notwithstanding, the state budget and
public services grew under the Reagan administration.

The times and personalities were different for the two Browns. Pat Brown
was governor at a time when California experienced unprecedented growth
and he responded by building the world's greatest educational system, thousands of miles of freeways, an elaborate water system, and significantly expanded social services. His son, Jerry, governed at a time when California (and
the nation) experienced slow economic growth and a backlash to unchecked
growth. Jerry Brown, trained as a Jesuit, did not believe in conspicuous con-

sumption, nor did he advocate for growth. He chose not to invest in California's infrastructure, hoping that fewer people would come to the Golden State. They came anyway.

Pete Wilson was handed a $10 billion budget deficit in his first year as governor. The state also suffered major fires, landslides, earthquakes, and one of the most severe recessions in its history during his eight years as governor. It is little wonder that he viewed the role of governor as that of "crisis manager."

Gray Davis approaches the governorship as a moderate and a pragmatist. In addition to moving the public agenda forward—education, public safety, rebuilding the infrastructure, economic growth—he wants to use the visibility and powers of his office to end what he calls "wedge-issue politics." Wilson was criticized for his positions on immigration and affirmative action. Davis wants to bridge the gender and race gaps, if possible.

Davis took office at a time when California experienced its "second gold rush." It is no wonder that he wanted to use his office to promote an "era of higher expectations." Gray Davis was Jerry Brown's chief of staff, but his approach to governing is very different from that of his former boss. Their different personalities and backgrounds undoubtedly explain their different leadership styles and philosophies of governing. But we should not underestimate the impact of the state's strong economy in the late 1990s, or the "just go for it" attitude of so many Californians during that time.

At least in the first two years of his administration, Davis seemed in a much better position to realize his ambitious goals than was his former boss, Jerry Brown. Circumstances changed for Davis with the energy crisis and the collapse of Internet-based companies. Davis has encountered other problems late in his first term in office. For example, no bid contracts were awarded to companies, such as Oracle, that contributed to Davis's very large campaign war chest. Davis's agenda during the last years of his first term had been lost in his mad dash to solve the energy crisis and respond to fund-raising scandals. His critics and the public alike gave him low marks for his approach to solving the energy problem (see Chapter 2).

THE PLURAL CHARACTERISTICS
OF THE EXECUTIVE BRANCH

The strange turn of events in the presidential election between George W. Bush and Al Gore raised serious questions about the electoral process. It also focused public attention on the critical role the president plays in uniting a divided nation. It remains to be seen if President Bush will be able to create a bipartisan atmosphere in Congress to avoid deadlock. While Bush faces a deeply divided Congress, he at least is fully in charge of the executive branch of government. This is not true for California's governor.

California's executive branch differs from the federal government in that it is a collection of independently elected officials. The state constitution requires the election of eight statewide officials and a five-member Board of

Table 6.1 Political Party of the Governor and Lieutenant Governor—1975 to 2002

Governor	Party	Lt. Governor	Party	Date
Edmund G. "Pat" Brown Jr.	Democrat	Mervyn M. Dymally	Democrat	January 6, 1975
Edmund G. "Pat" Brown Jr.	Democrat	Mike Curb	Republic	January 8, 1979
George Deukmejian	Republic	Leo T. McCarthy	Democrat	January 3, 1983
Pete Wilson	Republic	Leo T. McCarthy	Democrat	January 5, 1987
Pete Wilson	Republic	Gray Davis	Democrat	January 4, 1991
Gray Davis	Democrat	Cruz M. Bustamante	Democrat	January 4, 1999
Gray Davis	Democrat	Cruz M. Bustamante	Democrat	January 5, 2002

SOURCE: http://www.ltg.ca.gov/office_of/previousgovs/caltgovs.asp.

Equalization. In addition, the governor shares the executive power of this office with a number of boards and commissions.

A constitutional executive officer must be at least 18 years old a U.S. citizen, and a resident of California for no less than five years immediately preceding his/her election. Proposition 140 limits constitutional executive officers to two four-year terms. It also established term limits for other elected state executives, state legislators, and it reduced operational funding for legislators and it eliminated pensions for legislators elected after Proposition 140.[1] Earl Warren was the only governor elected to a third term prior to Proposition 140. He resigned midway through his third term to become chief justice of the U.S. Supreme Court.

If the primary goals of government are greater efficiency, flexibility, accountability, and responsiveness as suggested by the California Constitutional Revision Commission in 1996, then the state's executive branch is in need of restructuring.[2] The governor is significantly hampered in his ability to respond to the public agenda because he must share power with so many other elected officials.

Having the lieutenant governor run on a separate ticket from the governor further exacerbates the divided nature of the executive branch. This is an important difference between the state and national executive branches. The president and vice president are of the same political party and campaign together on the same ticket. The vice president is first selected by the presidential nominee, and not by popular vote. One consequence of the constitutional provision in California for the lieutenant governor to be elected by popular vote, independent of the governor, is that voters have elected governors and lieutenant governors of different political parties. While this has happened only seven times, it is significant that it has happened in five of the last six gubernatorial elections[3] (see Table 6.1).

The split ticket often leads to tension between the governor and lieutenant governor. This certainly was true for Jerry Brown, a liberal, and Lieutenant Governor Mike Curb, a conservative. Curb often threatened to use his executive authority powers as acting governor when Brown would leave the state to

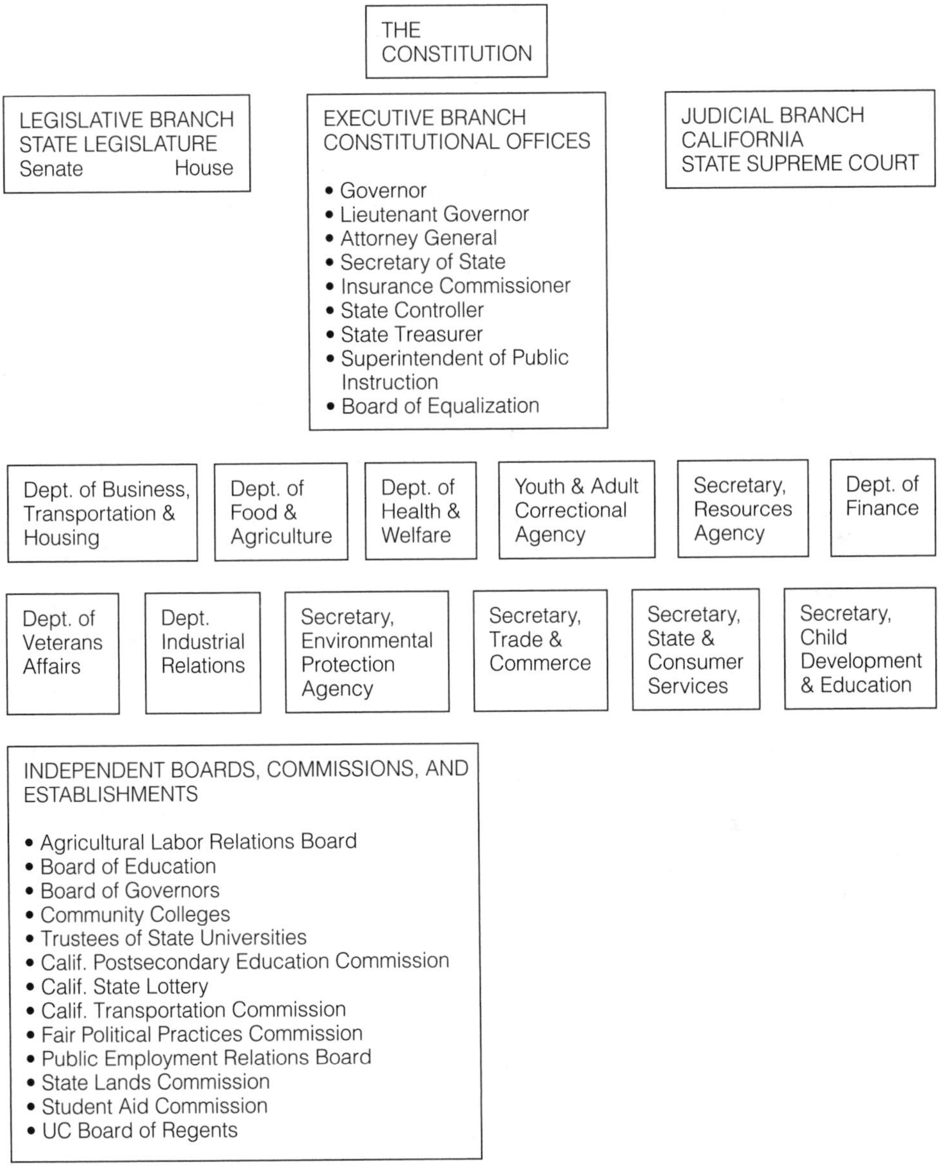

```
                          ┌──────────────┐
                          │ THE          │
                          │ CONSTITUTION │
                          └──────────────┘
```

| LEGISLATIVE BRANCH
STATE LEGISLATURE
Senate   House | EXECUTIVE BRANCH
CONSTITUTIONAL OFFICES

• Governor
• Lieutenant Governor
• Attorney General
• Secretary of State
• Insurance Commissioner
• State Controller
• State Treasurer
• Superintendent of Public
  Instruction
• Board of Equalization | JUDICIAL BRANCH
CALIFORNIA
STATE SUPREME COURT |

| Dept. of Business, Transportation & Housing | Dept. of Food & Agriculture | Dept. of Health & Welfare | Youth & Adult Correctional Agency | Secretary, Resources Agency | Dept. of Finance |

| Dept. of Veterans Affairs | Dept. Industrial Relations | Secretary, Environmental Protection Agency | Secretary, Trade & Commerce | Secretary, State & Consumer Services | Secretary, Child Development & Education |

INDEPENDENT BOARDS, COMMISSIONS, AND ESTABLISHMENTS

• Agricultural Labor Relations Board
• Board of Education
• Board of Governors
• Community Colleges
• Trustees of State Universities
• Calif. Postsecondary Education Commission
• Calif. State Lottery
• Calif. Transportation Commission
• Fair Political Practices Commission
• Public Employment Relations Board
• State Lands Commission
• Student Aid Commission
• UC Board of Regents

FIGURE 6.1. The Government of California

SOURCE: http://som.csudh.edu/fsmith/pub490/CALIFORNIA-EXECUTIVE%20BRANCH.doc. Used by permission.

campaign for the presidency. For example, Curb appointed a judge during one of Brown's campaign trips. Brown later rescinded the appointment. Why have the voters chosen to elect governors and lieutenant governors from different parties so frequently in recent years? Perhaps, as Gerston and Christensen argue, it is the result of weakened political parties in California.[4] Or, perhaps the voters simply want to put additional checks on the governor's powers.[5] It may also reflect a more divided electorate conflicted over difficult policy choices.

The elected officials that make up the plural executive branch of California government are the governor, the lieutenant governor, the attorney general, the secretary of state, controller, treasurer, the insurance commissioner, the superintendent of public instruction, the treasurer, the controller, and the board of equalization. (Figure 6.1 provides a chart of the executive branch.)

THE GOVERNOR

Similar to the president, California's governor serves as the chief spokesperson for the state. He is the supreme commander of the California National Guard. The National Guard can be activated to help in times of natural disasters or other emergencies. It also can be used to help quell civil disturbances, such as the student demonstrations in Berkeley during the 1960s or in Los Angeles during the Watts Riots in 1965 or the riots following the Rodney King verdict in 1992.

The governor is expected to set the public agenda—to lead. The state budget, known as an "executive budget," is the governor's most important tool for developing policy. The governor can reduce or eliminate items in the budget passed by the legislature through use of the line-item veto—a power bestowed upon the president in 1996. This veto power can be checked by the legislature and is subject to override by two-thirds vote of both chambers. The governor can also veto legislation subject to the same override provision. Historically, the veto has been a very powerful tool; since 1947, only seven gubernatorial vetoes have been overridden (George Deukmejian and Pete Wilson never had a veto overridden).

In addition, the governor presents his legislative agenda in January during his annual State of the State address. On the legislative, fiscal, and policy-making front, the governor can use the office to author initiatives. And on the judicial front, he can use his office to appoint justices to the courts.

The governor's explicit powers are somewhat diminished with the two-term limit imposed by Proposition 140. Second-term governors, with no opportunity for re-election, often find it difficult to influence those who are needed to further their policy vision—not unlike the president who also suffers "lame duck" status in his second term. On the other hand, Proposition 140 may have strengthened the hand of the governor vis-à-vis the legislature because he is dealing with younger, less seasoned legislators inasmuch as they have limited terms as well.

The governor shares some of his explicit powers with other branches of government. For example, while the governor is principally responsible for the fiscal health of the state, the legislature confirms the state's budget. The governor must submit a proposed state budget on or before January 10 of each year. The legislature has until June 15 to make whatever changes to the governor's budget plan it deems appropriate. The June 15 deadline has rarely been met in the past 20 years due to a weak economy and/or serious differences between

A Closer Look

Go to Governor Gray Davis's Web site (http://www.governor.ca.gov) and read his inaugural speech and his fourth State of the State speech to learn his agenda for California. You may wish to compare his inaugural address with that of his predecessor, Pete Wilson, to see the differences in their political philosophy. It is interesting to note the differences even between Wilson's first inaugural address and his second—based on changed circumstances in the state. You may wish to make the same comparisons between Davis's State of the State addresses.

Table 6.2 The Governor's Appointments: Who Must Confirm?

Positions	Who Must Confirm Governor's Candidate
Judicial: Appeals Courts and State Supreme Court	Commission on Judicial Appointments
Judicial: Municipal and Superior Courts (when vacated)	No one (valid until next scheduled election)
U.S. Senate (when vacated)	No one (valid until next scheduled election)
County Supervisor (when vacated)	No one (valid until next scheduled election)
Governor's personal staff	No one
Governor's cabinet	State Senate
Executive departments	State Senate
Boards and commissions	State Senate
Constitutional officers	State Senate
Board of Equalization	State Senate and Assembly

SOURCE: http://dl.ccc.ccd.edu/classes/internet/politicalscience100/midfinal/final-review/summary_C.

the Republicans and Democrats. Governor Davis and the legislature approved a budget on time during his first year in office because of a strong economy.

Although the governor has the power to appoint over five thousand people to state government positions including the courts, the Senate must confirm his appointees (see Table 6.2).[6] Political scientists Matthew Cahn and Eric Schockman point out that "with the exception of the removal of Supreme Court judges Rose Bird, Cruz Reynoso, Joseph Grodin in the mid-1980s, most judicial contests confirm incumbent judges and continue the gubernatorial legacy of their nominator."[7] (See Chapter 7 for a profile of Justice Bird.)

Independent Powers

The governor exercises powers independent of the other branches of government. Most notably, he oversees a large and complex bureaucracy made up of more than two hundred thousand civil servants and over sixty departments. The state bureaucracy is organized into nine "super" agencies: Business, Transportation, and Housing; Resources; Health and Welfare; State and Consumer Services; Trade and Commerce; Youth and Adult Corrections; Environmental Protection; Food and Agriculture; and Child Development and Education.

A gubernatorial appointee (referred to as a secretary) who provides the leadership and policy guidance of the current administration heads each of these super agencies. These agency heads serve as the governor's cabinet. Each of the super agencies oversees departments. For example, the Health and Welfare agency includes the departments of Social Services, Employment Development, Rural and Migrant Affairs, and Rehabilitation.

There are also three departments independent of the super agencies that report directly to the governor and that are part of this cabinet: Department of Finance, Department of Industrial Relations, and Department of Veterans Affairs. Cahn and Schockman report, "the executive heads of these agencies . . . play a key strategic role in determining how legislative public policy should or should not be implemented. There is wide policy discretion that cabinet officials may choose to follow as implementation orders filter down through the respective bureaucracy. The ultimate will of the sitting governor through these independent entities is felt throughout the governance of the state."[8]

There are numerous other agencies, councils, departments, and offices not grouped into a super agency, and the heads of which do not serve in the cabinet. Examples include the Military Department, Arts Council, and the Department of Information Technology. In addition, there are numerous independent commissions (perhaps the best known is the Lottery Commission) and education policy boards (see Figure 6.1). The governor can organize the administrative agencies of state government, subject to legislative veto.

Even though California government consists of a sprawling bureaucracy, the governor has remarkably few appointments compared to governors in other states. In the case of California, the civil service system has long been established for all but the top policy posts.[9] The goal of the state civil service system was the same as it was at the federal level—to award state government jobs based on merit and not on patronage. (See the section titled California's Civil Service System, later in this chapter, for a more detailed description of the state civil service system.)

The various boards and commissions, over which the governor has independent control, impact a wide range of policy arenas, including education, agriculture, utilities, and ethics as it applies to the electoral process in particular. A few of the more important commissions and boards are:

The University of California Regents. There are 18 members who are appointed by the governor and who serve 12-year terms. There are seven ex-officio members, and one UC student representative serving a one-year term. The regents are responsible for the nine campuses of the University of California.

The Board of Governors of the California Community Colleges. The governor appoints 16 members to the Board to serve four-year terms. They are responsible for overseeing the 71 community college districts, which are locally controlled.

A Closer Look

Go to http://CAL-ACCESS.ss.ca.gov to find out who gave how much money to Governor Gray Davis during his campaign and after. Pay particular attention to energy-related interest groups, given the energy crisis of 2001 in California. How much money, for example, did PG&E and Southern Edison Company give to the governor?

The Public Utilities Commission. The governor appoints this five-person Commission for six-year terms. The Commission regulates public and private utilities including gas, water, electricity, and telephone service.

The Fair Political Practices Commission (FPPC). The FPPC was created by the voters in June 1974 to enforce ethical reforms of the States Political Reform Act, covering, in part, campaign disclosures, lobbying activities, and legislator's election spending.[10]

Beyond formal powers, the governor wields considerable informal power as the chief spokesperson for the nation's largest state. He is the most visible elected official in the state and, as such, he can use the bully pulpit to mobilize public opinion in support of his public agenda. Even California governors with bland or boring personalities attract national attention by virtue of California's place in the Union. Pete Wilson is an excellent example of someone lacking in personal charisma, yet able to make a run for the presidency by virtue of his national prominence as governor of California.

While term limits, appointment confirmations, the detailed nature of the state constitution, and the plural nature of the executive branch all act to weaken the governor's power, it remains the most powerful position in state government.

OTHER STATE
CONSTITUTIONAL OFFICERS

The Lieutenant Governor

The lieutenant governor assumes the duties of the governor if he is temporarily or permanently unable to perform the duties of the office. A holdover from the days of more primitive methods of transportation and communication, the state constitution states "the lieutenant governor shall assume the duties of governor when the governor is off state soil." This provision, in combination with the plural nature of the executive branch, has sometimes allowed lieutenant governors to implement their own, often conflicting, agenda during a governor's travels out of state. Lieutenant Governor Mike Curb, a Republican, took delight in doing this while Governor Jerry Brown, a Democrat, traveled outside of California during his run for the presidency in 1980. A good example, as mentioned before, was Curb's attempt to appoint a judge during Brown's absence.

Like the vice president of the United States, the lieutenant governor has the largely ceremonial role of president of the state senate. The position gives the lieutenant governor a tie-breaking vote—this was last used in 1976. Unlike the vice president, whose responsibilities are largely delegated by the president, the lieutenant governor has some constitutional responsibilities. She or he is a member of various boards: an ex officio member of the Board of Regents of the University of California, chairperson of the Commission for Economic Development, as well as other boards and commissions.

The Attorney General

The attorney general is elected separately from the governor and is the chief law enforcement officer in the state. Because of citizens' concern for law and order, the position has often been a vehicle for successful gubernatorial campaigns.[11] Since the 1940s, for example, three attorney generals moved into the governor's mansion: Earl Warren, Pat Brown, and George Deukmejian.

The primary responsibility of the attorney general is to oversee the proper and uniform enforcement of the laws of California throughout the state. The attorney general is head of the Department of Justice and in this role is generally considered to be the second most powerful executive in the state. The attorney general and his or her office serve as legal adviser to the governor, other members of the executive branch, all state departments, and also important state boards and commissions. The attorney general oversees all district attorneys and sheriffs in the state.

The Secretary of State

Third in line to succession of the governor, the secretary of state is responsible for custody of public documents and records including the constitution. The secretary of state keeps correct records of the official actions of the legislative and the executive branches and is also charged with the custody of keeping all the acts and resolutions passed by the governor.

She or he is California's chief elections officer—responsible for administering the provisions of the elections code. The secretary certifies the nominations and elections of each candidate by ensuring that the necessary conditions for candidacy have been met. Also, the secretary is responsible for certifying the signatures on the petitions submitted for ballot propositions. He or she compiles the "Statement of Vote" after each statewide election, prepares the statewide elections voter guide, receives lobbyists' registrations and reports, and receives campaign contribution and conflict of interest disclosure statements. Finally, but no less important, the Office of Secretary of State is responsible for filing and maintaining articles of incorporation, registration of trademarks, and deeds to state lands. It also maintains the California State Archives and collects and indexes state government documents. The secretary of state is not usually considered a stepping stone to the governor's mansion. However, Jerry Brown used it successfully in the post–Watergate reform era.

The Controller

Sixth in line for succession, the controller is the chief fiscal officer of the state. The Office of the Controller is responsible for the accounting and disbursement of state funds; no money may be drawn from government accounts without the controller's authorization. This office oversees the fiscal affairs of the state, audits claims against state funds, administers inheritance and gift taxes, and performs a variety of functions assigned by the legislature, including publications of statistics on local governments.

The controller's office also has the following responsibilities:

Administers the payroll system for state employees

Chairs the Public Employee's Retirement System (CalPERS)

Chairs the State Teachers Retirement System

Chairs the Franchise Tax Board

Chairs the State Lands Commission and a dozen other state boards and finance commissions, including the Board of Equalization (to be discussed later)

The Treasurer

Different from the controller, the treasurer is responsible for the oversight of all the funds and securities belonging to the state of California. The treasurer functions as the state banker. In this capacity, the treasurer is responsible for selling and redeeming state bonds and investing surplus state funds. The treasurer pays warrants authorized by the controller and keeps accounts of all monies received and disbursed. In September of every other year, the treasurer reports to the governor the current balance of state funds as well as a summary of the sources and uses of funds over the previous two-year period.

The late Jesse Unruh used this office to obtain substantial financial contributions from Wall Street bankers anxious to do business with California, in order to finance his political ambitions. This office also provided a springboard for the unsuccessful gubernatorial bid for Kathleen Brown—the sister of former Governor Jerry Brown and the daughter of Edmond G. "Pat" Brown.

The Insurance Commissioner

The Office of Insurance Commissioner became an elective office in 1988 with the passage of Proposition 103. The commissioner is responsible for protecting the interest of insurance consumers in the state through regulation of the insurance industry. Supported by insurance fees, this office is responsible for enforcing the laws of the California Insurance Code. In addition, the insurance commissioner handles consumer complaints and certifies insurance companies who seek to engage in business within the state. No insurance company can do business in California without being certified by the insurance commissioner. All of this is accomplished through oversight operation by the state Department of Insurance.

Former Commissioner Chuck Quackenbush disgraced the office and raised serious questions about whether this sensitive position should be an elective office or appointed. In July 2000, Quackenbush was forced to resign to avoid impeachment. Quackenbush was accused of allowing six insurance companies to avoid billions of dollars in fines by donating $12.5 million to a fund he created. Ostensibly the fund was created to help victims of the 1994 Northridge earthquake and to study damage from earthquakes. However, none of the money was used for those purposes. Instead, approximately $6 million funded public service television ads featuring the commissioner, and the rest was donated to groups with little or no connection to earthquakes.

The Superintendent of Public Instruction

The superintendent of public instruction is the only elected member of the executive to run on a nonpartisan basis. The superintendent directs the Department of Education, which is responsible for implementing the policies set by the State Board of Education. The governor appoints the board. The superintendent is the ex officio director of education and a member of the Board of Regents of the University of California. In addition, the superintendent is the executive officer of the State Board of Education.

The Board of Equalization

The Board of Equalization consists of five members; four members are elected, and the fifth member is the state controller, who serves ex officio. The state is divided into four Board of Equalization Districts, with each district electing one member (for no more than two terms). A member of the board must be a resident in the district for at least one year preceding his or her election. The major duty of the board is to ensure equity and uniformity regarding the assessment of properties in all counties. In this sense, the board functions as a revenue agency in the assessment of property taxes and assesses the property of public utility holdings and railroads. It administers the retail sales tax, the cigarette tax, the fuel tax, and similar statewide taxes. From time to time, governors have proposed eliminating the Board of Equalization and the Franchise Tax Board (the state income tax agency) in favor of creating a Department of Revenue under the governor's control. To date, Governor Davis has not proposed such a change, nor is it likely to happen in the near future.[12]

THE STATE BUREAUCRACY
AND EFFORTS TO REFORM IT

How It Is Organized

A large staff assists the governor, with a chief of staff who supervises all of the governor's offices, acts as chief aide, and serves on the governor's cabinet. The governor also has an administrative officer, a press secretary, and various other assistants. However, the governor's chief source of advice is the cabinet.

Because the cabinet is the governor's primary source of advice, the governor has complete control over the composition of the cabinet, the length of time its members serve, and the level of importance its members play. While agency secretaries and department heads are the primary members of the cabinet, various other members may be invited to attend meetings when issues in their field are being discussed.

A director supervises the program and fiscal performance of each department. To create unity and cohesion among the many departments, each is grouped into one of the super agencies discussed earlier in the chapter (see Figure 6.2). A secretary who provides leadership and policy guidance for the departments within the agency heads each of the super agencies.

The agency secretaries also act as liaison between the departments and the governor in an effort to assist the governor in managing California's sprawling bureaucracy. However, on issues of importance, the governor may meet directly with the department heads.

California's Civil Service System

California adopted a civil service system in 1913. Like the U.S. civil service, the state's civil service requires that government jobs be awarded based on merit and not on the basis of whom you know. Prior to the state's civil service system, government jobs were often given to party loyalists or cronies—in what became known as the spoils system.

An important by-product of the civil service system is that public employees do not lose their jobs simply because a new party sweeps into office, bringing with it a new set of cronies or party loyalists. Consequently, not only are public employees presumably better qualified to do their jobs, but there is continuity in the state bureaucracy from election to election. California's civil service system was one of the results of the Progressive reform era.

Most state employees were part of the civil service system in the beginning. John Korey, a political scientist and expert on California politics, writes that over time, however, the system was weakened "through the creation of numerous categories of exempt and 'temporary' employees. . . . In 1934 a new article was added to the state constitution replacing the old Civil Service Commission with a State Personnel Board. The new board consisted of five members appointed for staggered ten-year terms by the governor with the approval of

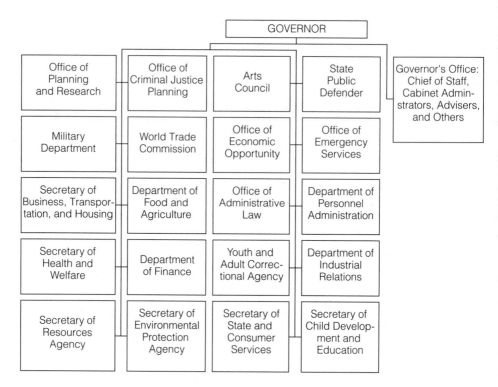

FIGURE 6.2. The Governor's Cabinet

the state senate. The number of exempt and temporary positions was sharply limited."[13]

Although the civil service brought to state government a level of professionalism and integrity unknown in the days of the spoils system, critics say it also resulted in an inflexible and, at times, unresponsive bureaucracy. Why? Because they enjoy tenure, civil servants are not compelled to support policy initiatives of the governor or his appointed department and agency heads. They will remain in their jobs long after the current administration and their appointed superiors leave office. This same complaint is often heard regarding the federal civil service system.

Proposed Reforms

Considering its importance, it is little wonder that the organization of California's plural executive branch has often provoked calls for reform. A central issue in the debates over how to reform the executive branch is the relationship between the governor and lieutenant governor. The California Constitution Revision Commission (CCRC), established by former Governor Pete Wilson in 1994, suggested ways to reform the state's executive branch, and chief among them was a way to change the relationship between the state's top two executives.

The CCRC's recommendations, reported in 1996, focused on improving accountability, responsiveness, and efficiency. In other words, any reforms should make clearer who is in charge of implementing state policy. While acknowledging that ballot propositions and initiatives limit the authority of the executive branch, the CCRC recommended the following reforms:

The governor and lieutenant governor should run on the same ticket in the general election and work as a team. The governor should be authorized to appoint the lieutenant governor to executive branch responsibilities.

The constitutional provision that transfers the governor's power to the lieutenant governor should be abolished.

The secretary of state, controller, and attorney general are important checks on gubernatorial power and, therefore, should continue as elective offices.

The superintendent of public instruction, treasurer, and insurance commissioner should be appointed by the governor, rather than elected, and subject to legislative confirmation.

Abolish the Board of Equalization, merge state tax administration functions, and create a tax appeals board (appointed by the governor and subject to senate confirmation). The regulatory and executive functions of the Board of Equalization, along with the functions of the Franchise Tax Board and other major revenue agencies, should be combined into a Department of Revenue.

Shorten the terms of the University of California Board of Regents from 12 to 10 years. Reappointment should be prohibited unless the appointee has served less than a full term. The number of appointed members should be reduced from the current 18 to 15. The superintendent of public instruction should be removed as a member of the board.

Shorten the terms and limit the functions of the State Personnel Board. The probationary and classification functions of the SPB should be transferred to the Department of Personnel Administration. The terms of State Personnel Board members should be shortened from 10 to 6 years.[14]

THE BUREAUCRACY:
RULES, REGULATIONS,
POLICIES, AND PROCEDURES

We learn in the next chapter that the legislature makes law. It is left to the bureaucracy to implement the law in the form of rules, regulations, policies, and procedures. Most laws are written in very general language, which leaves considerable discretionary authority to the various departments and agencies charged with carrying out the law. Simply put, agency or department regulations implement, interpret, or make specific the laws and policies established by the legislature or governor. It is for this reason that the bureaucracy has extraordinary influence over our daily lives. The State Parks Department, for example, establishes a long list of "dos" and "don'ts" for those visiting state parks. The ways in which laws are interpreted and implemented by the bureaucracy can frustrate legislators who may not agree with how their laws are being implemented.

The Office of Administrative Law (OAL) oversees the development of regulations to ensure that the public is not subject to illegal enforcement or to regulations that are incompatible with the policies that have been developed. The OAL, through the Administrative Procedures Act, ensures that the rules, regulations, and enforcement in various areas of government service at the state level are consistent with the original policies. State law takes precedence over regulations and policies.

An example of the governor's regulatory authority was when Davis issued an executive order on March 13, 2001, in response to the energy crisis. His order gave authority to regulatory agencies to suspend environmental and health requirements that are found to interfere with his order to build additional power plants. In this case, he determined that increased energy took precedence over environmental and health concerns.

A FINAL WORD

We wrote in the beginning of this chapter that every governor brings to the office his own style, political philosophy, and public agenda that, in part at least, reflects the times in which he lives. Even though the powers of the executive branch are divided among several elected officials and independent commissions and boards, it is the governor who is perceived by the people of California (and the nation) to be responsible for the state's economy, public safety, education, and related social programs. The governor, by virtue of personality and position, can mobilize public support for his policy initiatives. He also serves as the states liaison to other state, federal, and world leaders. To be elected governor of California in the modern age qualifies you to at least be considered as a viable candidate for the presidency—although only one governor, Ronald Reagan, has made it to the White House.

California's governor wields considerable constitutional power through the line-item and general legislative vetoes. He appoints hundreds of people to important judicial and administrative positions. In the end, however, the eventual success or failure of a governor ultimately rests with his ability to persuade and his good fortune to serve in times of prosperity. The rise or fall of a governor (much like the president) rests largely on circumstances—economic, social, and political—outside of his control.

ADDITIONAL RESOURCES

Governor Web site. Available at
http://www.ca.gov/t/governor.

Lieutenant Governor Web site. Available
at http://www.ltg.ca.gov.

Attorney General Web site. Available at
http://caag.state.ca.us.

Secretary of State Web site. Available at
http://www.ss.ca.gov.

Superintendent of Schools Web site.
Available at http://www.cde.ca.gov/
executive/index.html.

Board of Equalization Web site. Available
at http://www.boe.ca.gov.

General index Web site. Available at
http://www.ca.gov/s/search.

NOTES

1. The office of insurance commissioner
differs from other elected state executive
positions, however. Inasmuch as it was
created by statute, and not by the state
constitution, it is not covered by Proposition 140. Nevertheless, the statute that
created the insurance commission limits
the commissioner to two terms.

2. http://www.library.ca.gov/CCRC/
reports/html/hs-executive-branch.html,
Executive Summary, 6.

3. California Constitution Revision
Report, "Executive Branch," 1.

4. Larry Gerston and Terry Christiansen,
*California Politics and Government: A Practi-
cal Approach,* 6th ed. (Belmont, CA: Wadsworth, 2001).

5. Ibid.

6. Matthew A. Cahn and H. Eric
Schockman, *California: An Owner's Manual*
(Upper Saddle River, NJ: Prentice Hall,
1997), 15.

7. Ibid., 15.

8. Ibid., 16.

9. A.G. Block and Charles M. Price, eds.,
*California Government & Politics Annual,
1998–1999* (Sacramento, CA: Journal
Press, 1998), 3.

10. Ibid., 16.

11. See John C. Syer and John H. Culver,
Power and Politics in California (New York:
John Wiley & Sons, 1980), 130.

12. A.G. Block and Charles M. Price,
eds., *California Government & Politics
Annual, 1998–1999,* 4.

13. John L. Korey, *California Government*
(Lexington, MA: D.C. Heath and Company, 1995), 93.

14. California Constitution Revision
Commission (CCRC) Final Report, 1996,
7–8.

7

The Legislature

We open this chapter with profiles of two men who wielded unusual power in the lower house of the legislature, the assembly. They helped to shape California politics during most of the last half of the 20th century. They made the speaker of the assembly into the second most powerful position in state government—serving, in essence, as cogovernors. They were consummate politicians who knew how to get things done in Sacramento. While still an important position in the legislature, the role of speaker of the assembly has diminished since the glory days of Jesse Unruh and Willie Brown.

Jesse Unruh was elected speaker of the assembly in 1961. He was to remain in this powerful position until January 1969, when Republicans regained control of the lower house. He was speaker longer than any other person in the state's history, until Willie Brown broke his record by serving an incredible 15 years as speaker (1980–1995). Unruh served as speaker at a time when fundamental political change in the state and in the nation took place. As a result of several changes, including the "one person, one vote" ruling of the U.S. Supreme Court in 1962, and a shift in the state's population from rural to metropolitan areas, urban interests were more accurately represented. This meant that social and economic issues relevant to all Californians could now be introduced and discussed in the legislature. Society was undergoing profound turmoil and change. The Civil Rights movement had made a big impact on politics, and new attitudes about representation and equality were beginning to develop. Government was opened to greater scrutiny.

In this context, the strong-willed, able, and articulate Unruh felt the legislature—or at least, his house—should assume greater initiative and innovation in the legislative process. He introduced many significant changes in how the legislature conducted its business. The most important among these changes was to make it professional. Unruh felt that unless legislators were paid a living wage and worked full time, they would continue to be susceptible to the influence of lobbyists and would not see themselves as professionals, paid to represent their constituents. He pushed through a package of reforms, creating paid staff for representatives, and implementing a year-round legislature, making California's state government one of the most professional in the nation.

Some Unruh opponents argued that he used the ploy of improved legislative staffing to build up his own political organization for the future, but even they were quick to agree that the speaker had done more to improve the California Legislature than any man in the state's history. But Unruh was not content with these achievements. As speaker, he defied the tradition that a presiding officer does not carry legislation and introduced—year after year—an enviable legislative program of his own.

Affectionately called "Big Daddy," Unruh was unusually candid and open for a politician—he would tell it as it is. He is best known today for his insightful and still timely remark about money and politics: "Money is the mother's milk of politics." Toward the end of his career, he was quoted as saying, "If you can't drink a lobbyist's whiskey, take his money, sleep with his women and still vote against him in the morning, you don't belong in politics."

Willie Brown was the first African American Speaker of the assembly and, as noted, served in that role longer than any person—a record that will never be surpassed with term limits. Brown, like Jesse Unruh, used his position as speaker to become the most powerful Democrat in the state and to gain national prominence. Both Brown and Unruh made the speaker of the assembly into the second most powerful position in state government—second only to the governor.

Brown described himself as the "ayatollah of the state legislature." Biographer James Richardson describes Brown as the last great showman of the 20th century. He was flamboyant, a master at raising campaign dollars, and he knew how to get things done. "He used to essentially extort fabulous sums of money from business interests in the form of campaign contributions, under the implied threat that bills they wanted enacted (or blocked, in the case of the tobacco industry) wouldn't see the light of day if they didn't pay up. It was an efficient, smooth-running machine. Brown's genius was his ability to protect and expand liberal interests while buying off business interests with narrow favors. . . . Under Brown, the lobbying community became known as the "third house," since lobbyists were a de facto branch of the legislature. The biggest statist interests—the trial lawyers, the teachers union, and other labor groups—enjoyed a stranglehold on the legislature. Membership on "juice" committees—

banking, insurance, natural resources—was highly coveted because these committees allowed you to generate more campaign cash."[1]

THE LEGISLATURE
SUFFERS AN IMAGE PROBLEM

Of all the branches of state government, it seems the legislature is particularly vulnerable to criticism. Public opinion polls have shown consistently over the past few decades that the public sees it as inefficient, corrupt, and self-serving—not unlike their perception of Congress. The image of the California legislature was not always negative. As we mentioned, under the leadership of Jesse Unruh in the 1960s, the legislature was professionalized—full-time legislators, generous legislative salaries and perks, and ample expert staff. The California legislature was considered the best in the land by the early 1970s.

The voters expressed growing public disenchantment with the legislature when they passed Proposition 140 in 1990. Proposition 140 created term limits for California's elected officials and significantly cut the legislature's operating budget. Ken DeBow and John C. Syer, professors of political science and experts in California politics, interpret voter support of Proposition 140 as an indication that "professional politicians, and especially the professional legislature, were now seen as part of the problem rather than a positive source of solutions."[2] Many factors have hurt the legislature's image. Because of political infighting and petty bickering, it has repeatedly missed the constitutionally mandated deadline for submitting a budget to the governor. Although a strong economy helped the legislature deliver Governor Davis the FY 2001 budget on time, a rare occurrence during the past few decades.

A delay in reaching agreement on a budget causes a disruption of service, late payments to vendors and public employees, and ultimately a lowering of the state's credit. The legislature's image was also hurt by FBI sting operations in August 1988, which netted corrupt legislators. Nearly ten years later, the Speaker position in the Assembly was seriously weakened when term limits forced Willie Brown to leave office. The resulting power vacuum led to the Democrats failing to agree on who should replace Brown. A coalition of Democrats and Republicans eventually selected the new Speaker, but the position was forever weakened as a result.

In this chapter we describe the state legislature and the manner in which it works. In its structure and inner workings it is similar to that of the U.S. Congress and most other state legislatures. The chapter ends with a brief discussion of proposed reforms to make the legislature more efficient and responsive to the public. In thinking about reforms, we should consider what it is we want the legislature to do. Is its primary role to check the potential excesses of the executive branch, or is it to create good public policy? The answer will shape the institution.

A Closer Look

How do you view the California legislature? Do you think legislators generally are doing a good job? How would you rate the performance of the state legislature compared with the U.S. Congress? Do you know who your own representative is in the assembly? the state senate? Go to http://www.assembly.ca.gov/acs/acsframeset9text.htm and http://www.sen.ca.gov/~newsen/senators/senators.htp to find your representatives.

THE LEGISLATURE:
ITS STRUCTURE AND CHARACTERISTICS

Bicameral Legislature

The California legislature, similar to the U.S. Congress and 48 other states' legislatures, is bicameral (having two houses), consisting of the assembly and the senate. The assembly consists of 80 members, elected for two-year terms, and the senate consists of 40 members elected for four-year terms. Seats in both houses are apportioned on the basis of population. Following the 1991 reapportionment, the California Supreme Court ordered that every senate district be divided into two assembly districts. (See Table 7.1.)

Since the passage of Proposition 140 in 1990, the number of terms a legislator may serve has been limited. Members of the assembly are restricted to a maximum of three terms (six years) and senators are limited to a maximum of two terms (eight years). Half of the senators and all of the assembly members are elected in November of the even-numbered year in each election cycle.

Power in the assembly is concentrated in the hands of the speaker, while in the senate, it is more evenly shared among the various standing committees. Anyone who has been a resident of California for at least three years and a resident of a legislative district for at least one year preceding an election is eligible to run for and hold legislative office. Legislators in both houses are elected on a partisan ballot.

An Overview of Legislative Powers

The legislature is the policy-making branch of state government, restricted only by the federal and state constitutions, federal law, judicial rulings, and by the governor's veto. The legislature, through the passage of bills, creates the majority of state laws. Among the legislature's most important responsibilities are those relating to the budget and public finance. The legislature delivers a budget to the governor for signature, oversees spending, and levies state taxes. In addition to taxing and spending powers, the legislature has the authority to conduct investigations and ratify amendments to the U.S. Constitution. The senate confirms high-ranking, nonjudicial appointments made by the governor. Both

Table 7.1 Comparison of Federal and California Legislatures

	U.S. Congress		California Legislature	
	Senate	**House**	**Senate**	**House**
Number of members	100	435	40	80
Term of office (years)	6	2	4	2
Term limit	None	None	2 terms (8 years)	3 terms (6 years)
Term limit	Vice President	Speaker	Lieutenant Governor	Speaker

SOURCE: http://Thomas.loc.gov/home/legbranch/legbranch.html and http://www.leginfo.ca.gov.

A Closer Look

Go to http://www.ncsl.org/programs/ legman/about/terms.html to learn more about the impact Proposition 140 has had on the legislature. What are some of the positive and negative effects on the legislature?

---

houses may reject the governor's nominations for vacancies in any of the state's constitutional offices.

Lower House: The Assembly

The speaker of the assembly is the primary source of leadership and power. Though its power has diminished since the days of Jesse Unruh and Willie Brown, whose political skills and abilities to raise large sums of campaign dollars for fellow legislators has been unmatched by their successors, it remains the most important position in the assembly. The speaker, a member of the majority party, is elected by a simple majority of its members. There are, however, times when the speaker gains a majority of votes with the help of the minority party. For example, Willie Brown, a Democrat, was elected with the help of 27 Republicans in 1981, and Doris Allen enjoyed a brief tenure as speaker with the help of Willie Brown and his fellow Democrats in 1995.

The speaker has the power to appoint all committee chairs and vice chairs, including the all-important and powerful Rules Committee. The speaker must also approve all subcommittees formed to help the committees in their work. The speaker is empowered to appoint a majority of any committee, legislators who are in agreement with his or her views on particular subjects.

The speaker has other important powers, including scheduling committee meetings and referring bills to committees. Both of these responsibilities influence how legislation is handled in the assembly. For example, if a committee meeting to consider a particular bill is held at odd hours or in conflict with other meetings, that bill's fate can be significantly affected. In addition, depending on the committee to which the speaker assigns a bill, the bill's fate can vary from receiving strong support to never seeing the light of day.

Noel Stowe, a professor of history at the University of Southern California, suggests how the speaker's power in assigning bills to committee might be important to the eventual outcome of a piece of legislation.

The Agriculture Committee or the Labor, Employment, and Consumer Affairs Committee might study a bill dealing with agricultural labor. One committee might react more favorably to legislation favoring growers, while the other might be likely to support a strong measure in favor of farm workers. Thus the decision as to which committee receives the measure for study has everything to do with the kind of bill that eventually will be presented to the assembly for final vote.[3] The speaker also exercises considerable influence on the floor of the assembly by virtue of his or her authority to conduct floor sessions. In this role, the speaker uses parliamentary rules and procedures to control the flow of debate and to influence the final vote on a bill. The speaker controls much of the assembly's operation. Thus, if the speaker is solidly against a bill, its supporters usually have the choice of either seeing it fail or of modifying it to gain his or her acceptance. This situation does not mean that the speaker controls every bill or even cares to do so. However, if the speaker chooses to take a stand on a particular bill, his or her position will probably prevail.

When the powers of the speaker's office are in the hands of leaders like Willie Brown or Jesse Unruh, who were willing and able to use these powers to their fullest extent, the assembly behaves quite differently than when the speaker is someone less adroit in matters politic, or less prone to use their powers. Because of the interparty and intraparty fighting in selecting a successor to Willie Brown following the 1994 elections in which the Republicans gained control of the assembly, the speaker's position was considerably weakened. Doris Allen, for example, was unable to wield much control over her own party members, let alone the assembly as a whole.

The Ways and Means Committee is the most important committee in the assembly. It serves as a general clearinghouse for most bills before they reach the floor—a function not unlike that of the Senate Finance Committee (to be discussed). Every bill that has fiscal implications (all the important bills) must first go to the Ways and Means Committee before it goes to the floor.

Upper House: The Senate

The presiding officer of the senate is the lieutenant governor, who has very little actual power other than to cast the deciding vote in the case of a tie. The lieutenant governor does not vote on any other measures, introduce bills, or, for that matter, attend very many daily sessions of the senate. The senate elects a president pro tem, the most influential member of the senate. The president pro tem, usually the leader of the majority party of the senate, acts as a substitute in the lieutenant governor's absence and is also the chairperson of the Senate Rules Committee.

The Senate Rules Committee is very powerful because it appoints all other senate committees, designates their chairperson and vice chairperson, and assigns bills to these committees. Although being a member of the Senate Rules

Committee is a powerful position in the senate, it does not have the same level of power as that of the speaker of the assembly. Unlike in the assembly, power in the senate is shared more evenly among committees and other senators.

The Budget and Fiscal Review Committee and Appropriations Committee are also very important. Drafting the budget is largely the responsibility of the Budget and Fiscal Review Committee. Because the Appropriations Committee hears all other bills with direct or implied state costs, it has the power to kill most major bills.

Compensation

The job of a California legislator went from part-time work, with little pay, staff, or office space, to full-time work in 1966. The pay and working conditions improved, along with the enhanced responsibility. How did it come to pass that the California Legislature became a full-time job, and the highest paid legislature in the country? Prior to 1966, state legislators were required by the state constitution to work 120 days for general sessions in odd-numbered years and 30 days for budget sessions in even-numbered years. Their annual pay was only $6,000, and they operated with inadequate office space and with very few professional staff.

Proposition 1A, approved by the voters in 1966, revised the state constitution and was the first step in modernizing the state legislature. Proposition 1A, approved by the voters in 1966, revised the state constitution and was the first step in modernizing the state legislature. The voters acknowledged it was a full-time job to legislate in a state as large and complex as California. Passage of Proposition 1A not only made each year's legislative session unlimited but also raised the pay of legislators to $16,000 and allowed them to grant themselves 5 percent annual cost-of-living increases. However, Proposition 112 in 1990 revoked this power.[4] Today, legislators earn $99,000 annually, plus $25,000 in tax-free living expenses paid to those who reside more than 50 miles from Sacramento.[5] The leadership of the legislature receives additional pay. The speaker of the assembly and president pro tem of the senate each earn an additional 15 percent of their annual, base pay. The majority and minority leaders of both houses earn 7.5 percent above their annual salary.

Legislators do not have a retirement system. Proposition 33 was soundly defeated by the voters in the 2000 elections. This proposition would have allowed legislators to voluntarily participate in the state's retirement system. Only veteran legislators (and they are dwindling in numbers thanks to term limits) were "grandfathered" in under the original legislative retirement system.

An additional step toward modernizing the state legislature was taken in 1972, when voters approved a constitutional amendment that established the same two-year schedule for the state legislature that holds for the congress—with bills remaining alive for two years. The legislature operates on year-round basis, with breaks for Easter, Christmas, part of the summer, and during state-wide elections.[6]

Staffing the Modern Legislature

State legislators, like members of congress, depend a great deal on their staffs for drafting legislation, advising them on how to vote on a particular bill, responding to inquiries from their constituents back home, and much more. In 1990, a total staff of approximately 2,500 served the legislature. Compare this to the less than 500 staff that served the part-time legislature in 1966. It is true that with the passage of Proposition 140 in 1990, mandating budget reductions for the legislature and term limits, the staffing was reduced significantly—down to approximately 1,800. However, this number still reflects a major increase since 1966.

Among the legislative staff are three positions that deserve special attention. They are the legislative counsel, legislative analyst, and the auditor general. These three staff serve the entire legislature; whereas all other staff members work either for individual legislators or on behalf of one of the houses. The 200-member legislative counsel includes over 80 lawyers. They assist the legislature in drafting and evaluating the constitutionality of all bills. The legislative council must provide a digest of every bill identifying the changes a proposed bill would make in the law, before it can be introduced. The legislative analysts give advice to the legislature on all major bills with fiscal implications.[7] The top priority of the analyst is to study the governor's budget (known as the "executive budget") in an attempt to make state government more efficient. Consequently, the analyst works to identify cuts in the governor's proposed budget. The legislative analyst also prepares analyses of ballot propositions that appear in the voter pamphlets mailed to all registered voters prior to an election. The auditor general, a certified public accountant, conducts financial audits of state agencies. The purpose of the audits is to ensure that agencies spend money for the purposes intended when the legislature appropriated the funds.

THREE TYPES OF LEGISLATION

The main business of the legislature comes in three forms: bills, constitutional amendments, and resolutions. A legislator is the only one allowed to introduce these measures. The governor must turn to a friendly member of the legislature to introduce a bill on the governor's behalf. Even the governor's budget must carry the name of a legislator, as is true with all legislatures in the United States.[8]

A bill is a proposal to change, repeal, or add to an existing state law. A bill can be introduced in either the senate, known as a senate bill (SB), or the assembly, known as an assembly bill (AB). A bill needs a majority vote of both houses and approval of the governor to become a law. However, if the bill is an "urgency measure" or involves an appropriation of funds, then a two-thirds vote is required. Most bills originate with interest groups, staff members, constituents, or other government officials.[9]

A constitutional amendment is in the form of a resolution proposing a change in the constitution and can originate in either the assembly (known as an ACA) or the senate (known as a SCA). Passage of a constitutional amendment requires the two-thirds vote of the members of each house. When a constitutional amendment is proposed, it must be approved by a majority of California voters before it can take effect.[10]

There are three types of resolutions that may be passed by the legislature: concurrent, joint, and house. Both houses use a concurrent resolution to adopt joint rules or to establish joint committees. A concurrent resolution needs only a majority vote to pass. The joint resolution, which can be introduced in either house, urges the passage or defeat of legislation pending before the U.S. Congress or presidential action.[11] A house resolution expresses the sentiments of that house, either the senate or the assembly. This type of resolution must be adopted by a majority in one of the houses and is often used to amend a rule or create a committee within that specific house.[12] Resolutions are normally passed by voice vote. Unlike bills, neither constitutional amendments nor resolutions are subject to gubernatorial veto.[13]

The legislature handles at least five thousand pieces of legislation during each two-year session. Those who are interested in tracking all of the proposed legislation during this period may turn to three sources published by each house: the *Daily File,* the *Daily Journal,* and the *Weekly History.* The key to use any of these sources is to know the specific bill number and the session of origin. These documents are available on the Internet.[14]

HOW A BILL BECOMES A LAW

Mark Twain said "There are two things one should never watch being made: sausage and laws." Humor aside, it is important to understand the steps involved in making state law. The first step is for an individual legislator to introduce a bill (see Figure 7.1). When first introduced, the bill's title is read, and the bill is printed. Next, the bill is assigned to a committee by the speaker in the assembly, and by the Rules Committee in the senate. In most cases, legislators do not write the bills they introduce. Bills often originate from sources outside the legislature, such as lobbyists, private citizens, the executive branch (remember, the governor cannot introduce a bill directly), and local government agencies. As a result, the legislature spends a considerable part of its time on proposed legislation that has different starting points within the network of California government.

The most critical stage for most bills is when they are reviewed in legislative committee. During committee consideration, the chair of the committee often exercises a number of options to aid in the consideration of the bill. The chair may, for example, refer the bill to a subcommittee of the committee for further review. The chair may also send copies of the bill to executive departments or agencies for their opinions and reactions. If the bill is of great impor-

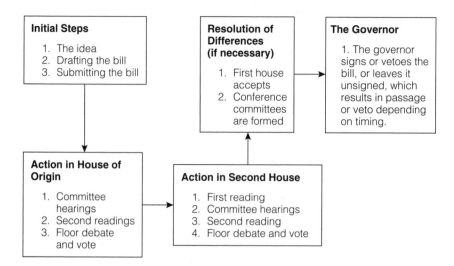

FIGURE 7.1. How a Bill Becomes a Law

SOURCE: The Center for Continuous Study of the California Economy, California Economic Growth, November 1995, p. 26. Used by permission.

tance or of a highly controversial nature, the chair may call for pubic hearings on the bill to allow all interested parties an opportunity to comment.

The committee can recommend passage of the bill, with or without proposed amendments; it can report the bill out of committee without recommendation, which sends it forward; or it can table consideration of the bill, which usually spells the bill's death. The great majority of bills introduced in the legislature, many of which are written to benefit small interest groups, are in fact tabled in committee.

When a bill is reported out of committee, its title is read a second time. Any amendments proposed by the committee and from the floor of the house in which it is read are voted upon at that time. The bill is then reprinted with all of its approved amendments and placed on the agenda for debate. Floor debate can only end by a majority vote of those present. Once debate has ended, one of three things can occur: the bill may be passed, the bill can be rejected, or the bill can be sent back to committee. Committees attempt to resolve serious opposition through amendments prior to reporting a bill out of committee.

The senate vote is taken by roll call and recorded by the secretary of the senate. Once roll call is concluded, members may not change their votes and absent members may not add their votes. The assembly uses an electronic vote counter. Upon unanimous consent of the membership, members may change their votes the same day, or absent members may add their votes if doing so will not change the outcome.

Both houses require a simple majority vote to pass an ordinary bill. There are some measures that require a two-thirds majority in both houses: override of a governor's veto; budget bills; bills with an "urgency clause"; constitutional amendments; and bank, corporation, and insurance tax bills. Urgency clauses require immediate action for reasons of public need or safety. Urgency bills go into effect immediately. The 1993 Workers' Compensation Reform Act, for example, contained several urgency clauses, including antifraud measures. If the bill passes by the necessary majority, it is sent to the other house, where a similar process takes place. Both houses must pass the same version of the bill before it can be sent to the governor for consideration. If signed into law, most bills do not take affect until the first of the following January. The exception to this rule is those bills with an "urgency clause"; as implied in the name, the situation would require immediate attention.

A conference committee is formed when a different version of the same bill is passed in each house. This situation happens when a bill approved in one house, for instance the assembly, is sent to the senate (in this example) and is amended. If the assembly does not approve the bill as amended by the senate, a conference committee of three members of each house is formed to reach a compromise version of the bill. Approval of the budget prior to sending it to the governor always requires a conference committee. It is common practice to follow this procedure toward the end of a legislative session in an effort to handle last-minute bills in a speedier fashion. A conference committee report is prepared more quickly than "a revised printed version of a bill." [15]

If both houses approve a bill, it is sent to the governor for final action. The governor has several options depending on the nature of the bill and when he receives it. If the governor approves the bill, it is signed into law and becomes effective 90 days after the adjournment of the legislature. A bill may also become law if the legislature is in session and the governor fails to sign it within 12 days of receiving it.

If the governor opposes the bill, it can be vetoed and returned to the house of origin. The bill is also vetoed if the legislature adjourns within the first 12 days that the governor has the bill and the governor refuses to sign it after a waiting period of 35 days. Finally, if the bill is an appropriations bill, the governor may reduce or eliminate a specific appropriation (without vetoing the entire bill) through the line-item veto. The legislature can override a gubernatorial veto with a two-thirds vote of each house, but this has been extremely rare in California legislative history. [16]

EFFORTS TO REFORM THE LEGISLATURE

Californians want state government to perform more efficiently and effectively. Although there is little agreement on specific reforms, public opinion polls, low voter turnout, and support for propositions like 140 — term limits— indicate that the public is not happy with the status quo.

The legislative branch is a particularly easy target for criticism. The process by which a bill becomes a law is cumbersome, and, more important, it is vulnerable to "interest group politics" and political infighting. The simple fact is, many of the political structures and processes that worked in the early days no longer work. Bill Hauck, chairman of the California Constitutional Revision Commission, commented,

> In a state of 31 million people, the largest in the nation, the fundamental question is how can we achieve greater efficiency in government and accountability from our elected representatives. This question is central to the work of the Constitution Revision Commission. . . . The objective is to bring government closer to the people, so that functions, financing, and responsibility are much clearer. In such an organization, it will be more understandable who is responsible for which government services or programs. [Bill Hauck, CCRC News, California Constitution Revision Commission, February 1995, 1]

The commission offered four bold recommendations in its Final Report issued in 1996:

- Lengthen the limit on legislative terms of office to three four-year terms in each house. The terms can be staggered so that one-half of each house is elected every two years. Implementation of this provision should be done so that no current member of the legislature can benefit.

- Shorten legislative sessions to six months per year and commence legislative action on a bill within ten days of its introduction.

- The legislature should be given the constitutional authority to review and reject administrative regulations.

- After revising the legislative terms of office as recommended in number one, legislators should be able to participate in the regular Public Employees Retirement System (Proposition 33 in the 2000 elections offered this option to legislators, but it was rejected by the voters).

The commission felt strongly that these changes would streamline the legislative process and reduce gridlock in Sacramento, but no substantive action has occurred on the first three recommendations. The voters in the 2000 elections, as we mentioned, defeated the fourth. No wonder Mark Twain once commented, "No one is safe while the legislature is in session."

A FINAL WORD

Jesse Unruh helped to make the state legislature a professional and nationally respected body. In the process, he transformed the speaker's position into the second most powerful position in state government, second only to the governor. He was politically astute, spoke his mind, raised millions of campaign dollars in support of himself and those loyal to him, and championed many liberal causes while in the legislature, and later as state treasurer. He was affectionately called "Big Daddy."

Willie Brown, on the other hand, was known as the "ayatollah of the state legislature"—reflecting Brown's iron fist approach to ruling the assembly as its speaker. Like Unruh, Brown knew how to get things done, using his considerable prowess as a fundraiser, his uncanny ability to find others' weaknesses, and his power of persuasion. You may not have liked the politics of either Unruh or Brown, but even their critics had to admire their ability to move legislation.

Since the days of these two political giants, the legislature is less well regarded by the voters and its national reputation as a well-run legislative body is tarnished. FBI stings and subsequent scandals, weakened leadership (particularly in the Speaker position), and several budget impasses in the years of economic downturns contributed to infighting and petty bickering among legislators. Years of legislative ineffectiveness were the result.

The California voters' response to the scandals and perceived ineffectiveness of the legislature was Proposition 140 and term limits. Simply put, the voters no longer trusted their legislators to act in the public's best interest. Are legislators more responsive to the public, or more honest, as a result of Proposition 140? The jury is still out. However, some argue that it is now more difficult for legislators and their staffs to serve the public because term limits force experienced and talented law makers to leave office prematurely (Willie Brown is a prominent example). A reduction in legislative staffing does not help either. Legislators depend on their staff to research and write legislation, as well as analyze proposed legislation drafted by lobbyists and their fellow legislators.

The energy crisis and faltering state economy will challenge the legislature to better manage its internal affairs so that it can respond to the external threats confronting this great state. Decisive, honest, and thoughtful leadership will be essential.

ADDITIONAL RESOURCES

General Internet resource: http://www
.leginfo.ca.gov.

Senate: http://www.senate.ca.gov.
Assembly: http://www.assembly.ca.gov.

NOTES

1. http://www.reason.com/9712/fe
.hayward.html.

2. Ken DeBow and John C. Syer, *Power and Politics in California,* 6th ed. (Boston: Allyn & Bacon, 1997) 133.

3. Noel Stowe, California Government: *The Challenge of Change,* 2nd ed. (Encino, CA: Glencoe Publishing Co., 1980), 139.

4. In 1990, a constitutional amendment (Proposition 112) was approved, which, among other things, created the Citizens'

Compensation Commission. The commission now establishes pay raises for the legislature, thereby taking the heat off of the legislators.

5. *San Francisco Chronicle,* March 16, 1999, A13.

6. Thomas A. Hoeber and Charles M. Price, eds., *California Government and Politics Annual 1995–1996* (Sacramento, CA: Journal Press, 1996), 33.

7. Michael J. Ross, *California: Its Government and Politics,* 3rd ed. (Pacific Grove,

CA: Brooks/Cole Publishing Co., 1987), 155.

8. Hoeber and Price, eds., *California Government and Politics Annual, 1995–1996,* 32.

9. Ibid., 30.

10. League of Women Voters, *Guide to California Government,* 14th ed. (Sacramento, CA: League of Women Voters of California, 1992), 36.

11. Ibid., 37.

12. Ibid., 37.

13. Hoeber and Price, eds., *California Government and Politics Annual 1995–1996,* 32.

14. See http://www.leginfo.ca.gov/ senate-journal.html and http://www.sen .ca.gov/~newsen/schedules/files.htp for examples.

15. Hoeber and Price, eds., *California Government and Politics Annual 1995–1996,* 32.

16. Ibid.

8

The Judiciary

In the matter of capital punishment in California, many felt that Chief Justice Rose Bird and her court chose to override the will of the people in blocking 68 death sentences before she and two of her colleagues were voted out of office in 1986. Justice Bird let stand only four death sentences during her ten years as chief justice of the California Supreme Court.

While many attribute her defeat in the 1986 election to her opposition to the death penalty, not all agree. In her obituary (she died of cancer in December 4, 1999) penned by the American Civil Liberties Union the case is made that "her purported opposition to the death penalty was not the motivation for conservatives who set out to remove the state's first female Supreme Court justice from office, rather it was the club they used to punish her for other trespasses. California's re- newed death penalty statute (1976) and Justice Bird (1977) burst on the scene about the same time. The new Bird Court had the task of examining the constitu- tionality of a brand new, and in many legal scholars' estimation, badly drawn state law expanding the use of the death penalty. Her court's rulings, necessary to refine the law and protect the constitutional rights of the accused, overturned most of the death sentences brought before it."

While there may have been other reasons why conservatives wanted Justice Bird off the court, there is little doubt that it was her record on capital cases (and that of Justices Cruz Reynoso and Joseph Gordin) that motivated voters to turn her and her two colleagues out of office. The death penalty enjoyed strong public support in California during her tenure, as it does today.

Justice Bird once said, "My role isn't to be politically smart. My role is to do what's right under the constitution. And if that's politically unpopular, so be it." She also said, "It is easy to be popular. It is not easy to be just." [1] *In the words of Chief Justice Ronald M. George:*

> *Chief Justice Bird was a trailblazer as the first woman to serve on the Supreme Court, that now has three women among its seven members. She made many contributions to the administration of the California court system and the Supreme Court in particular. Among other things, Chief Justice Bird appointed the committee to implement Proposition 32, which changed the court's procedures for granting cases for review, and oversaw the implementation of its recommendations.*
>
> *The first computers were instituted at the court during Chief Justice Bird's tenure. She also established the Committee on Gender Bias in the Courts just before leaving office in 1987. That committee was expanded by her successor, Chief Justice Malcolm M. Lucas, and provided a report and recommendations that continue to be implemented statewide today. She also was an early supporter of state funding for the trial courts, since implemented throughout California. As a jurist, she was a strong and eloquent advocate for her views.* [2]

ROLE OF THE COURTS

Judicial power in the state rests with the state supreme court, appellate courts, superior courts, and municipal courts. The general responsibility of the courts is to provide a means to settle disputes, determine the guilt or innocence of those accused of violating the law, and protect the rights of individuals from the state.

The courts—or the judicial branch of state government—interact with both the legislative and executive branches of government, as is true for the federal government. The legislature develops laws, which often affect the operations of the courts. The courts are linked to the executive branch through the governor's many important judicial appointments.

As discussed in the first chapter, the California constitution is far more detailed than the United States Constitution. The executive and legislative branches, therefore, have far less power than the president and Congress. As a result, some scholars believe that the California state judiciary may be even more powerful since it is charged with interpreting the detailed California constitution. [3]

THE COURT SYSTEM

The California court system is structured in a hierarchical manner (see Figure 8.1). It is helpful to think of the courts as divided between trial courts and appellate courts. Superior courts, municipal, and justice courts are considered trial courts. The state supreme court and the courts of appeal are classified as

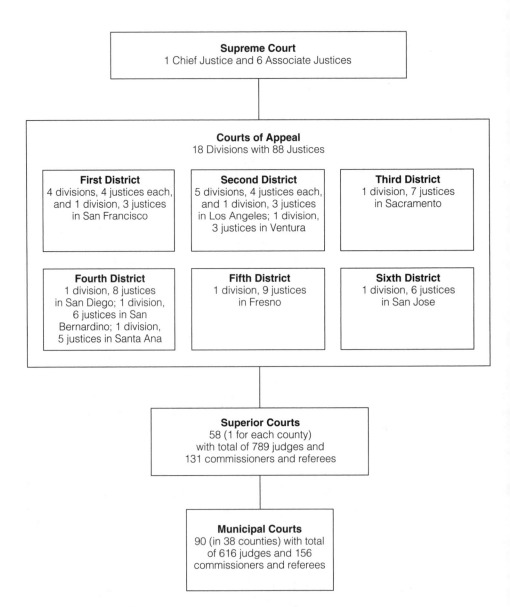

FIGURE 8.1. The California Court System

appellate courts. The different levels of the state judiciary are discussed below in their order of importance from least to greatest.

Municipal Courts

These local courts hear civil cases involving $25,000 or less, criminal cases, and misdemeanors. On matters involving $5,000 or less, these courts can act as small claims courts, where attorneys are not required.

Superior Courts

These are countywide courts that hear juvenile cases, felonies, appeals from municipal court decisions, and civil suits involving more than $25,000, and other cases such as those dealing with wills and estates. Superior courts also handle child custody and divorce cases. Juvenile cases are typically heard as civil proceedings, even when they deal with criminal offenses. Every county must have at least one superior court.

Unified Superior Courts

Proposition 220, adopted in June 1998, permits counties to unify their superior and municipal courts, and their respective functions. The goal of unified courts is to achieve countywide efficiencies in operation and caseload management. Unification of the two court systems in each county required approval of judges in those counties. All 58 counties had voted to unify their municipal and superior court operations by January 2001.[4]

Courts of Appeal

There are six appellate districts located in San Francisco, Los Angeles, Sacramento, San Diego, Fresno, and San Jose. The appellate courts vary in the number of justices (see Figure 8.2), but normally only three justices will hear an appeal. A decision requires that two of the three justices agree in a case. Cases from these courts can be further appealed to the state supreme court, provided that the supreme court agrees to hear the appeal. Few cases, however, make it to the supreme court—similar to the U.S. Supreme Court. These courts also have jurisdiction over appeals from superior court actions as well as decisions of quasi-judicial state boards.[5]

The Supreme Court

The Supreme Court is composed of a chief justice and six associate justices who are all appointed by the governor, subject to confirmation by the Commission on Judicial Appointments, *not* the senate (see Figure 8.3). The state's highest court handles appeals from the district courts of appeal, although some cases can be taken directly from the trial court to the supreme court. In death penalty cases, for example, appeals automatically go from the superior court to the supreme court. In addition, the supreme court reviews orders of the Public Utilities Commission (PUC) and has some appointive powers.

Jury System

California uses a standard jury system. Grand juries (composed of 19 jurors in most counties, 23 jurors in Los Angeles County) investigate public agencies and can hand down criminal indictments. The state supreme court ruled in 1978 that preliminary, or probable cause, hearings must be held, whether or not a suspect is indicted. This ruling applies, however, only to felony cases.

First District	Second District	Third District
4 divisions, 4 justices each, and 1 division, 3 justices in San Francisco	5 divisions, 4 justices each, and 1 division, 3 justices in Los Angeles; 1 division, 3 justices in Ventura	1 division, 7 justices in Sacramento

Fourth District	Fifth District	Sixth District
1 division, 8 justices in San Diego; 1 division, 6 justices in San Bernardino; 1 division, 5 justices in Santa Ana	1 division, 9 justices in Fresno	1 division, 6 justices in San Jose

FIGURE 8.2. California Courts of Appeal

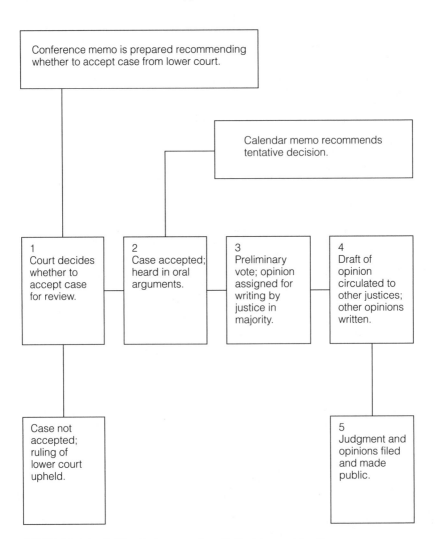

FIGURE 8.3. The California Supreme Court's Decision-making Process.

SOURCE: "The California Supreme Court's Decision-Making Process," *Los Angeles Times,* November 23, 1978, part 1, 3. Used by permission of Tribune Media Services International.

A Closer Look

What lessons can we learn from the O.J. Simpson trial in terms of jury selection? Did the location of the trial make a difference in the pool of potential jurors?

A preliminary hearing is an opportunity for the judge to decide if there is probable cause to remand a case to superior court for trial. It is not very difficult, in most cases, for the prosecutor to prove probable cause because the burden of proof is very low in a preliminary hearing. An alternative to a preliminary hearing is an indictment by a grand jury. Grand juries, however, are seldom used in California.

Trial juries usually consist of 12 registered voters. Both the defense and prosecution can agree to a smaller jury or waive the right to a jury and submit the case to a judge. A unanimous vote is needed for acquittal or conviction in a criminal case.

JURY SELECTION

Most attorneys agree that one of the most important phases of a trial is jury selection. In fact, many will argue that it is the most important part of a trial. An example that is often cited to support this claim is the O.J. Simpson trial. It is for this reason that attorneys rely on consultants who specialize in developing psychological profiles on prospective jurors—if the defendant can afford to retain their services, that is. Selecting jurors who are likely to be sympathetic to their side is a big part of the courtroom battle between prosecutors and defense attorneys.

The judge just prior to the start of a jury trial requests a panel of prospective jurors. Prospective jurors are first sworn to tell the truth prior to their being questioned by the prosecutor and defense attorney. The process during which potential jurors are asked questions, first by the judge and then by the prosecution and defense attorneys, is called voir dire. Potential jurors may be excused by either side for cause or peremptory reasons. An unlimited number of jurors may be excused for cause. Each side is limited to 10 preemptory challenges in most criminal cases (20 in death penalty cases).

APPOINTMENT, ELECTION, AND REMOVAL OF JUDGES

Justices on the supreme court are all appointed by the governor, subject to confirmation by the Commission on Judicial Appointments (consisting of the chief justice, the attorney general, and a senior appeals court judge). Not surprisingly, governors, when making appointments to the various courts, often select attorneys who have been helpful in their political careers. Governors also look to attorneys who are rated highly by the State Bar Association. Qualifications for chief justice include admission to the California State Bar and at least ten years' tenure as a judge.

It is not automatic that the governor's nominee is confirmed. For example, when Governor Jerry Brown nominated Rose Bird in 1979 to fill the vacancy left by Donald Wright, a controversy erupted. Rose Bird's appointment was opposed by leading conservatives in the state because they (and others) considered her to be far too liberal and inexperienced in judicial matters. The Commission on Judicial Appointments confirmed her, however.

Prior to 1979, governors were known to select judges on the lower courts for reasons other than their qualifications, e.g., in return for political favors. Legislation was passed in 1979 requiring judicial nominees first be evaluated by the State Bar Association before being appointed by the governor. In turn, the state bar created the Commission of Judicial Nominee Evaluations (19 members elected by the state bar and 6 appointed by the governor) to perform the evaluations. Even if the JNE rates a nominee as unqualified, however, the governor still may appoint his person.

Supreme Court justices must stand for confirmation by the people in a plebiscite in the first general election after their appointment is confirmed. A plebiscite calls for the electorate to vote for or against the governor's choice. If the voters reject the justice, then the governor must nominate someone to fill that seat on the court. If the voters approve the justice, then he or she must be reconfirmed in a general election every 12 years. Rose Bird and her two colleagues, Justices Cruz Reynoso and Joseph Grodin, are evidence that re-election to the state's highest court is not automatic. It is rare, however, that incumbent justices are defeated.

During the late 1970s and early 1980s, the state supreme court had a reputation for being an activist court, involving itself in controversial decisions. Governor Brown continued to make the court more representative by appointing Bird, the first woman to serve on the state supreme court, and also the first Latino, Cruz Reynoso, and an African American, Allan Brousard.

Former Governor Pete Wilson appointed the current chief justice, Ronald George, an associate justice in 1991. He also appointed Janice Rogers Brown as an associate justice in 1996. She is the first African American woman on the court. She is also the first justice to be rated unqualified by the Commission on Judicial Nominees. She was found to be unqualified because of her limited judicial experience and her predilection to interject politics into her opinions.[6]

Currently, the state Supreme Court justices are:

Chief Justice: Ronald George

Associate Justice: Marvin Baxter

Associate Justice: Janice Brown

Associate Justice: Ming Chin

Associate Justice: Joyce Kennard

Associate Justice: Stanley Mosk died in June 2001; Governor Davis appointed Federal Judge Carlos R. Moreno to fill the vacancy on September 26, 2001

Associate Justice: Kathryn Werdegar

In thinking about gubernatorial appointments to the courts, especially the state supreme court, it is interesting to speculate on the type of appointments Governor Gray Davis might make when he is given the opportunity. The last Democratic governor to appoint a supreme court justice was Jerry Brown, in late 1982. Since then, we have had Republicans in the governor's office for 16 years. Predictably, the court system swung from liberal to conservative, as the Republican governors were able to replace Brown's liberals with more conservative justices. What will Gray Davis do? After all, he was Jerry Brown's chief of staff and grew up (politically, anyway) under Brown's tutelage.

It is doubtful that Davis's appointments will swing the courts in a radically new direction—certainly not to the degree that his mentor did during his eight years in office. Davis is a strong law-and-order man, for example. He supports the death penalty. In this area of the law, he is not that different from his Republican predecessors. On the other hand, he is considerably more liberal on matters of the environment and labor-management relations. He also will not be likely to appoint pro-life justices. What we can say is that whomever Davis appoints will likely be a Democrat. Judicial appointments are highly partisan. Rarely will a governor appoint an attorney from the opposite party. Consequently, as Mona Field, a professor of political science and an elected official in California government, and Charles P. Sohner, professor emeritus of political science, argue, "after 16 years on the outside, there's a big backlog of Democrat attorneys who would like to be judges, and sitting Democrat trial court judges itching to move up the judicial ladder. At least until 2003, it's now Republican judge hopefuls who are frozen out."[7]

The process for nominating, evaluating, and confirming justices works the same way for the district courts of appeals as it does for the state supreme court. However, the process for filling the superior and municipal courts works differently. Judges in each of the 58 superior courts, as well as municipal court judges, are elected by the people in the respective jurisdictions for six-year terms. The governor fills any vacancies. On occasion, there is an open race for a judgeship, but this is a rare occurrence. Usually, the governor has filled the position before election day. The advantage of incumbency works on behalf of judges, just as it does for politicians. In other words, appointed judges almost always win in the next election.

The Commission on Judicial Performance

Any judge at any level may be censured, removed, or otherwise disciplined by the state supreme court, if the Commission on Judicial Performance recommends such action. The Commission on Judicial Performance is composed of:

Three judges appointed by the supreme court

Two lawyers elected by the state bar

Six "public" members

Two appointed by the governor

Two appointed by the speaker of the general assembly

Two appointed by the president pro tem of the senate

Judges are also subject to impeachment and recall. However, this is less
common.[8]

OVERSIGHT OF THE JUDICIAL SYSTEM

Administration of the court system is the responsibility of the State Judicial
Council. Judicial councils were created in several states as part of a reform
movement in 1926 to improve the quality of justice by improving court practices. Ronald M. George, chief justice of California and chair of the judicial
council, and William C. Vickrey, administrative director of the courts, write,

> The Constitutional amendment creating the Judicial Council authorized
> the Chief Justice to assign judges from less encumbered courts to those
> carrying the heaviest caseloads, to 'equalize the work of all judges.' This
> practice provided only a temporary solution to a growing problem, how-
> ever. Three reforms during this period helped ease court workload pres-
> sures: the establishment of the Fourth District of the Court of Appeal, the
> creation of new trial court judgeships, and the expansion of the jurisdic-
> tions of some lower courts. [Ronald M. George and William C. Vickrey,
> *Profile: Judicial Council of California* (Sacramento, CA: Administrative
> Office of the Courts, 2002), 2]

> The State Judicial Council is composed of 21 members:

> Chief justice of the state supreme court

> Fourteen judges appointed by the chief justice

> Four judges elected by the state bar

> One member chosen by the assembly

> One member chosen by the senate[9]

The Administrative Office of the California Courts is the staff agency
charged with carrying out the State Judicial Council's policies and conducting

Box 8.1 Public Opinion and the Judges: How Much Linkage Do We Want?

In the federal judicial system, judges, once appointed, serve for life. The only form of removal is impeachment, generally reserved for those who actually violate the law. But in California, as Rose Bird and two of her high-court allies discovered, judicial job security is not so ironclad. Unpopular decision can mean the end of a career.

Some have argued that California judges, just like their federal counterparts, need complete independence from the voters if they are going to be able to do their jobs, which include upholding the law against popular but unconstitutional ideas and protecting unpopular minorities against a "tyranny of the majority."

Others argue that in a day and age when judges make public policy just like any other politicians, voters should have a right to remove them when those policies consistently deny the public what it wants. Why should judges be insulated from voters just because they wear black robes?

Should California adopt the federal model and grant life tenure to its judges? Should we subject our highest court judges to more frequent elections with actual candidates running against them? Or is the current system of long terms interrupted by retention votes rather than competitive elections about the right mix between judicial independence and judicial accountability?

What do you think?

SOURCE: Debow and Syer, *Power and Politics in California*, 203.

research for the council. The council's responsibility is to continually provide oversight at all levels of the state judiciary system. It makes recommendations to both the governor and the legislature based on research conducted by the administrative office of the California courts. In addition, the administrative office promulgates rules and regulations regarding court procedures and administration.

One of the immediate challenges for the Judicial Council is to continue its efforts to provide greater public access to the courts and ensure fairness in the administration of justice. Technology will be an important tool in meeting this challenge. In the short term, "the council is considering a recommendation that the state assume full financial responsibility for 460 court facilities in California, a significant number of which need repair, renovation, or maintenance. The council also is eager to develop integrated court technology systems that will allow coordination among courts, law enforcement agencies, and other parts of the justice system."[10]

PROBLEMS WITH THE COURT SYSTEM

The judicial system suffers from a number of problems. First, not all persons selected to judgeships are qualified. Second, California lacks an effective system for removing justices who are incompetent or worse. Third, qualified justices often exhibit political passion, which can prevent them from being confirmed, or cost them their bid for reconfirmation (Rose Bird is an excellent example). Fourth, the courts are inundated with more cases than they can handle expediently. Finally, accountability in the administration of the court system is another issue that needs to be addressed.

Many people criticize the selection process. They maintain that judges are often selected on the basis of their politics, when what citizens need are the most qualified people and not just those who adhere to the policies of the governor. Unfortunately, the most qualified people often do not seek judgeships, as they can make far more money as private attorneys.

The U.S. Constitution guarantees all citizens a speedy public trial. However, because of an overcrowding of dockets, the backlog in the system can lead to extended delays—up to three years in a civil suit. It is not clear that merely creating more courts and appointing more judges would provide a practical solution. One proposed solution known as alternative dispute resolution (ADR) would have civil cases go to mediation first and then to the courts only if the parties are unable to resolve their disputes.

A FINAL WORD

The court system is not a passive branch of state government. Many laws passed by the legislature end up being tested in the courts. Often the courts themselves implement policy through their decisions. It is therefore important that judges are both qualified and responsive to the public voice while adequately protected from the momentary passions of shifting political winds. Former Chief Justice Rose Bird is an excellent example of someone who was willing to render decisions that overturned popularly supported laws that may not have been constitutional.

The judiciary may be viewed as the most powerful of the three branches of California government. One source of its power is the fact that the state constitution is so detailed, restricting the other two branches of government in ways the U.S. Constitution does not limit the presidency or Congress. Furthermore, the state supreme court has the power to strike down acts of the legislature or propositions passed by the voters if they are found by the high court to conflict with the state constitution. Finally, the courts can use their power to void acts of the executive branch that violate a statute or the constitution.

ADDITIONAL RESOURCES

Cain, Bruce E., and Noll, Roger G. 1995. *Constitutional Reform in California: Making State Government More Effective and Responsive.* Berkeley: Institute of Governmental Studies Press, University of California.

California Court system Web site. Available at http://www.courtinfo.ca.gov.

Recent court decisions: http://www.california.findlaw.com.

NOTES

1. http://www.bemorecreative.com/one/1060.html.

2. http://www.coutinfo.ca.gov/newsreleases/NR78-99.html.

3. A.G. Block and Charles M. Price, eds., *California Government & Politics Annual, 1998–1999* (Sacramento, CA: Journal Press, 1998), 18.

4. Governor's Budget Summary 1999-2000, 172-173.

5. Block and Price, eds., *California Government & Politics Annual, 1998–1999*, 20.

6. *San Francisco Chronicle,* January 26, 1996, A19.

7. Mona Field and Charles P. Sohner, *California Government and Politics Today,* 9th edition, (Boston, MA: Allyn & Bacon Publisher), 168.

8. Block and Price, eds., *California Government & Politics Annual, 1998–1999,* 20.

9. Block and Price, eds., *California Government & Politics Annual, 1998–1999,* 9.

10. George and Vickrey, 14.

9

California's Local Units of Government

One of the most crucial issues faced by all local governments, particularly for cities and counties, is that of growth. Achieving a balance between enough growth and too much growth is very difficult to do. Growth is an extremely salient issue for citizens and frequently forms the crux of many battles over the future of communities—more economic and job development versus preservation of current values and aesthetics of communities. These battles are hard-fought since they involve not just political issues but citizens' most deeply held values. Among other organizations interested in this issue, the California League of Cities has adopted a ten-point plan for Smart Growth that addresses some of these difficult issues for local governments. This plan includes maximizing existing infrastructure, encouraging active city centers, coordinating regional developments, emphasizing joint use of facilities, and encouraging citizen participation.[1] The political battles over issues like growth and the subsequent attempts to manage them by local government officials are interesting and important.

Practitioners and observers of all political persuasions tend to agree on one thing: California has a complex system of local units of government (LUOG) with a multitude of responsibilities and authority. Indeed, California residents may be surprised to learn that they reside in several different jurisdictions at once.

The decisions made at the local level by local policy-makers often have the most direct impact on residents since local responsibilities are extensive and include our direct services. The more familiar services include public safety (fire fighting, police, and emergency medical response), education, and zoning. However, other services, such as job training, welfare, court systems, and detention are also locally based but are less well known.

Local jurisdictions do not always act alone. They interact with each other, with special districts, with the state, and even with the federal government in many important ways. These interactions create vertical and horizontal relationships that are known as intergovernmental relations (IGR).[2] Most Californians probably find it difficult to understand which level of government is responsible for providing a particular service. Among the states' politicians and public administrators, the issue is often about which level of government should pay for the services provided.

The relationships among these entities is often shifting and confusing. Counties provide most of the health and human social services to their citizens but get much of the funding to do so from other levels of government. The passage of Proposition 13 had the effect of shifting power and money from local governments back to the state. Since Prop 13's passage, the voters have been reluctant to approve increased taxes or fees. Together, these factors have led to long and difficult battles over finances between the different levels of government. As mentioned in Chapter 5, new battles over the budget are being created as the state seeks to balance its budget by transferring services (but not funds) to counties.

TYPES OF LOCAL GOVERNMENT
UNITS AND THEIR ORGANIZATION

There are many different types of local government units within California. These include:

- Counties
- Cities
- City-county combinations
- School districts
- Community college districts
- Special districts
- Local agency formation commissions (LAFCOs)
- Regional governments
- Joint Exercise of Powers Act—Working together via contracts

As stated by the State of California Legislative Analyst Office, "Most Californians are governed by several overlapping local governments: a city, county, school, and community college district, plus one or more special districts."[3] Still, Californians have fewer local government jurisdictions than do citizens in many states (see Table 9.1).[4]

Table 9.1 Local Government Units in California

Type of Jurisdiction	Number Existing in California
Counties	58
Cities	474
Redevelopment Agencies	400
Special Districts	4,787
K–12 School Districts	986
Community College Districts	72
Total	6,777

SOURCE: Legislative Analyst's Office, 2002. CAL-Facts: California's Budget and Economy in Perspective. http://www.lao.ca.gov/2000_reports/calfacts/ 2000_calfacts_state-local.html

A Closer Look

In how many different jurisdictions do you reside? Which ones are they? Ask around and check the blue pages of your phone book for listings of all different jurisdictions in your area. Which ones overlap?

Each of these and their general purposes and organization will be described in this chapter, beginning with counties.

Counties

California has 58 counties: some operate under general state law and others by charters (similar to a constitution). (See the section on cities for an explanation of these legal terms.) County government, as a legal entity in California, is older than city government and was first used by the state as its primary unit of local government.

Boards of supervisors, which are usually elected by district, govern counties. In most counties, the board appoints a chief administrative officer (CAO) to supervise the details of county government administration. Counties also have other directly elected and appointed officials with specific governmental powers (see Table 9.2). It should be noted here that, although public health is typically a county function, the city of Berkeley maintains its own public health department and performs these functions as a municipal responsibility.[5] Counties also provide municipal services to those unincorporated areas of a county—those areas that are not officially considered a city. Many counties use special districts or contract with the California Division of Forestry for fire protection services.

Geographically, the largest county is San Bernardino and the smallest is San Francisco (which is also a city, the only combined city-county in the state). In

Table 9.2 County Officials and Their Jobs

County Official or Department	Job Description or Function
District attorney	Prosecutes legal cases
Sheriff	Arrests, detains, incarcerates, and monitors parole activities
Assessor	Assesses or values all real property for purposes of property tax revenue generation
Treasurer	Manages the revenue collected
Tax collector	Collects the taxes determined by the assessor
Public health	Conducts inspections, disease control, medical, mental and substance abuse services, care for the indigent and poor, and the county (general) hospital
Social services	Implements welfare, food stamps, custody, employment training, and other forms of public assistance
Public works and transportation	Builds and maintains roads, bridges, mass transit, water, sewer, waste disposal, and public buildings and related improvements
Officials for libraries, museums, parks, and other cultural or recreational venues	Manage the agencies that run the libraries, museums, and parks and recreation
Clerk or recorder	Registrar of voters, recordings of births, deaths, marriages, divorces, and transactions involving real property
Legal counsel	Acts as legal adviser
Auditor-controller	Accounts for public spending.

terms of population, Los Angeles County is the largest with over nine million people while Alpine County has just 1,200.

For some of the services provided by counties, like social services and public health, the county functions as an administrative arm of the state government. The state government establishes the rules of the program, funds the program, then passes onto the county the responsibility and the funds to administer the program. This is the essence of intergovernmental relations and a major reason that citizens often have difficulty in identifying where in California government to turn to on matters of personal interest. The situation is similar for programs funded by the federal government by grants directly to the counties.

Both the state and the federal government oversee county governments and their activities through the reports that counties make when they receive grants, through financial audits, and through citizen feedback to elected representatives. Successful administration on the county level requires interagency administrative skills, acceptance of central rule-making by the state or federal government, and program design emphasizing uniformity in task performance and measurement.[6]

Court operations present a unique category. Chapter Eight detailed the structure of the judiciary in California. Specifics regarding authority for services, location, construction, and funding trial operations can and frequently do change annually. This also applies to the organization and governing of these "lower" courts.[7] Detention or incarceration is both a county and a state function. There are county detention facilities, state prisons, and the California Youth Authority for juveniles. The past several years have seen an increase in the number of statutes imposing fixed and mandatory sentences on an increasing number of crimes. This has led to an increase in the costs of the court system as well as prisons at both the county and state levels. Clearly, the criminal justice system is a shared state and county partnership. Independently elected officials influence this partnership: state office holders, legislators, county office holders and judges. Justice may be blind but it certainly requires a feel for intergovernmental relations.

California voters have approved various propositions that have had an impact upon county finances. In 1994, they approved Proposition 172, establishing a ½-cent sales tax increase in the state constitution specifically for local public safety. However, in 1998, Proposition 218 restricted the ability of local governments to raise revenue through fees and assessments. Also in 1998, counties were designated to receive new amounts of money from increased cigarette and tobacco product taxes provided by the passage of Proposition 10. A portion of the funds received from the November 1998 nationwide settlements of litigation against tobacco companies (states participating in the litigation were to receive $206 billion over 25 years plus independent settlements with four other states led to an additional $40 billion over 25 years) are due to go each year to county health departments so this may also ease their fiscal stress.[8]

Overall, the financing of county services has been described as dysfunctional. While the demands for county services increase, the revenue sources to pay for them are often plundered by the state, limited by decisions made beyond county level control or constrained by yet another ballot initiative. Journalist Noel Brinkerhoff comments, "As a result of what has come to be known as 'ballot-box budgeting' over the past 20 years, California has developed a system of finance for local governments that frustrated officials describe as piecemeal in design and disincentive in motivation."[9]

While this certainly applies to all California local governments, it is a particularly appropriate observation about the primary administrative arm of the state government—the county.

Cities

California has about 475 incorporated cities. Under a general rule of American law called Dillon's rule, cities are officially "creatures of their states." Therefore, they can only do what their states say that they can do. About 385 cities are jurisdictions that operate under a structure that is established by specific state law. The remaining cities operate under a general set of rules and operational principles that are established by city charters; the principles in these charters are laid out under state law as well.

If a community chooses to incorporate into a legal city, there are two ways: general law and charter. A general law city is a community that operates under certain general conditions specified by the state. (Unincorporated communities that operate under general law have services provided to them by the county or through special districts.) A charter city is an incorporated city that chooses, by majority vote of its citizens, to operate under a charter document—akin to a small constitution. The procedure for incorporating a community into a city involves the Local Agency Formation Commission (LAFCO). LAFCO determines whether a proposed plan for incorporation is feasible. It can approve or deny a community petition for incorporation. If approved, an election is held and a simple majority of voters living in the area of the proposed city will result in a "new" city or LUOG.

Cities can grow in two ways: annexation and consolidation. First, land contiguous to the city may be annexed; a proposal for annexation must have the approval of the LAFCO and the governing body of the city. If the territory to be annexed is inhabited, a petition for annexation, signed by at least 25 percent of the qualified voters, must be filed with LAFCO. If LAFCO approves the petition, the city council must conduct a public hearing, at which time the issue is discussed. Annexation requires a simple majority voter approval within the annexation area and an approval from LAFCO.

The other form of growth, consolidation, occurs when two or more cities merge to form one larger city. Again, a simple majority vote is needed in all cities involved.

Within the framework of general law or charter, cities operate under one of the following systems:

Strong mayor system. Under the strong mayor system, the mayor is the chief administrative officer (CAO) of the city, and policy is set by the city council. Strong mayor systems tend to occur more often in larger cities.

City manager system. The city manager system (also known as a weak mayor or council-manager form of government) is the most common form of city government in California. Under this system, the mayor is elected by the people or the city council and acts as the ceremonial chief of the city. Often, the mayoral position simply rotates among members of the council. The administration of municipal affairs is under the control of a powerful city manager or administrator, professionally trained for public or city administration. The city council has the power to appoint and remove the manager and set overall municipal policy. The state constitution gives city voters initiative, referendum (through the council), and recall powers. Ukiah is believed to have had the first city manager form of government in the United States.

California does not have a legal definition of a town. Small communities that perceive themselves as towns organize to provide services under the county structure as either a county service area or community service district. Both types of organization can be created by written request to the county board of supervisors by 10 percent of the registered voters. A board of supervisors governs a county service area. A community service district selects a board of directors through election or appointment. In addition to these county-created forms of local governance, communities can organize collectively under a corporate charter. An example of a community organized under a corporate charter is Pebble Beach in Monterey County, home of the well-known golf courses.

California cities generally provide the following services:

Public safety (police and fire protection)

Recreational facilities

Street maintenance

Refuse pickup and disposal (including recycling)

Water supply

Sewage

Zoning (can be divided into planning, community development, permits and inspections in larger cities)

To provide these services, cities raise their own revenue through taxes and fees. These services are typically administered by professional administrators under the supervision of the city manager or strong mayor and with the policy guidance of the city council.

Some cities also have commissions and boards to oversee various other obligations of the city. These other obligations and services can include:

- Airports, ports, and harbors
- Public and low income housing
- Redevelopment and urban renewal
- Culture, historical, and parks
- Economic development

Cities are not sovereign. They are creatures of the state. Therefore, they must enforce state laws and codes and can see their authority preempted by the state (e.g., fireworks regulation and smoking ordinances). The state also returns revenue to cities through the provisions of Proposition 13 and in specific areas such as the gas tax, which is used for mass transit and street construction and maintenance. Also, cities use a complex system of federal grants for a variety of municipal purposes: community development and facilities, mass transportation, redevelopment, and housing—to name just a few.

However, in an intergovernmental environment, cities do not act independently. In some areas, smaller cities cooperate with one another to provide services, while in other areas they do not cooperate but instead duplicate services that are also provided by other nearby jurisdictions.[10] In other areas, they work together.

Cities and counties have a special relationship due to their proximity and overlapping natures. Both provide their services through departments or by contracting out. While both cities and counties have unique responsibilities, they also work together very closely. Like coordinated members of a relay team, cities rely on the county to assume some responsibilities such as law enforcement but to play some role in the overall administration of some local government functions. Counties generally provide large, regional facilities (such as parks), while cities provide neighborhood locales and programs. Likewise, counties often use city programs as reasons or purposes to justify their services and facilities.

In addition, counties and cities are allies in the efforts to halt the state's ability to usurp their property tax earnings. In order to prepare for possible losses of property tax revenues, counties and cities have become increasingly dependent on sales tax earnings and the kind of retail-heavy development that fosters such revenue at the expense of communities without large retail establishments.

Innovations in managing services. To manage local services, California cities have been among the first and the most innovative governments in the country in using technology to enhance efficiency and citizen service. The cities of Palo Alto and San Carlos in Silicon Valley were the first two cities to have a Web presence and continue to pioneer online services by themselves and in partnership with other jurisdictions in the Smart Valley Project (which developed innovative ways to allow citizens to obtain building and other permits online).

Santa Monica, through its Public Electronic Network (PEN), had an Internet presence long before the World Wide Web. Through PEN and its original text-based conferencing system, citizens talked with one another and organized to create projects like SWASHLOCK, a facility that provided showers, washing machines, and lockers for the homeless.

Sunnyvale pioneered the development of performance measures that allowed governments to track how effectively they were providing services to their citizens. They then worked studiously to pass on the lessons they learned to other local jurisdictions and to the federal government, which used many of their ideas in their efforts to reinvent and reorganize federal agencies.

Many, many other jurisdictions in California have been engaged in interesting and innovative projects that improve services for their citizens. These efforts serve to improve California government and public policy for everyone.

City-County Government

San Francisco is a combined city-county local government unit operating under a charter. As a completely consolidated city-county government, the City/County of San Francisco provides both county and city services to its citizens. There are no other cities or unincorporated areas in the county. The city/county is governed by a mayor and a Board of Supervisors.

San Francisco is not alone in this arrangement. There are other consolidated city-county combinations around the country and in Canada. Miami–Dade County, Nashville, Indianapolis, and Toronto have all adopted some form of city-county consolidation. Typically, the purpose is to reduce the complexities of overlapping jurisdictions and the higher costs of duplicated services. These arrangements are also attempts to capture the economies of scale and to take advantage of the added purchasing power possessed by larger jurisdictions.

> ## A Closer Look
>
> By using a World Wide Web search engine, find your own community's Web site. What services are available there for you to use? Using the Web site as a starting place, see if you can find some innovative ways that your local governments are providing services to you and your neighbors.

School Districts

In order to provide education services directly to its citizens, California has about 1,200 school districts for public schools from kindergarten through grade 12. These school districts operate as independent districts with directly elected school governing boards. The chief administrative officer is typically the school superintendent, a professionally trained administrator with specialized knowledge in education administration.

Much of local politics centers around school boards and education issues, and schools are often the centers of their communities. Schools also can serve as unifying institutions, bringing citizens together to discuss and organize around issues important to their children. Many politicians got their start by running for their local school boards or working with their local parent-teacher association.

Funding for local school districts is a continuing issue. Under the federal Serrano v. Priest case, the state is required to subsidize local schools in order to ensure equal per-pupil spending across districts. Since Proposition 13, school districts have had to rely heavily on the state in the wake of declining local revenues. This reliance was enhanced when Proposition 98, passed in 1988, guaranteed a minimum level of state funding for K–12 and community colleges. School districts also rely heavily upon property taxes to support their programs, but there are still districts every year that are in a deficit situation.

In addition to distributing funding for schools, the state has become increasingly involved in local education issues. Governor Gray Davis made education a continuing priority of his administration, frequently stating that it is his first, second, and third priority. Former Governor Wilson also emphasized education and made decreased classroom size for lower grades a reality before he left office. These lowered class sizes are at a risk in many districts in 2003 as they strive to solve their budgetary problems.

Community College Districts

Community college districts also operate as independent districts with directly elected trustees. Placed strategically throughout the state, community colleges provide freshman and sophomore courses with minimal fees. The main goal of these systems is to provide accessible, affordable education to Californians who

---

A Closer Look

Using the local phone book, your newspapers, local property tax bills, and informed sources, see if you can find out in how many overlapping jurisdictions you live.

---

want to take advantage of these opportunities. Like K–12 school districts, community college districts rely heavily on the state for funding.

Special Districts

California has more than 3,400 special districts, jurisdictions formed to provide a specific service to a specifically defined geographic area. Examples range from large regional districts such as the Metropolitan Water District in Los Angeles to the local mosquito-abatement districts (like the Marin/Sonoma Mosquito and Vector Control District, the first organized district in California).

Many cities are too small to adequately handle a certain service. Or, sometimes a particular geographic area has specific issues in need of government response. Such instances are best handled by formation of a special district that can adequately administer and finance provisions for a governmental response.

Special districts usually finance their services through an assessment practice of some kind. Directors are elected by district voters govern special districts. A general manager usually oversees administration. Directors who are elected by district voters to govern special districts. A general manager usually oversees administration.

Many of these special districts are virtually invisible to voters, even though voters elect the directors and pay taxes to support the services of these districts. This creates a serious problem of accountability to the citizens of California and the rest of the country. Officials and administrators who are largely unknown are making decisions about transportation, health, and other crucial issues. The solution to this problem? Citizens need to watch their tax bills and election ballots very carefully—they may be voting and paying for services of which they are unaware!

OTHER TYPES OF LOCAL ARRANGEMENTS

In addition to the local jurisdictions discussed above, there are several other types of arrangements and organizations that can have immense impact upon local governments in California. These include Local Agency Formation Commissions (LAFCOs) and regional agencies.

Local Agency Formation Commissions

All 58 California counties, including the combined City/County of San Francisco, have a commission that serves as a clearinghouse for annexation of territory by a local agency within the county as well as the creation of new cities in unincorporated areas of the county. This agency is called the Local Agency Formation Commission, whose existence was authorized in the 1963 legislative session to deal with the problem of overlapping and fragmented jurisdictional boundaries around the state. This legislation was reformed in 2000. The role of the LAFCOs is to review proposals for the creation of new governmental agencies in order to help ensure that boundaries and agency missions are coordinated and do not overlap, to reduce urban sprawl, and to subsequently help to preserve agricultural land.

The membership of each LAFCO differs by county, but most have two members from their Board of Supervisors and two members from the city councils in their county. Some also have members from independent districts and a member of the general public.

Regional Agencies

There are numerous limited-purpose regional agencies in California. Two types of these regional associations exist—those that deal with specific policy and governmental issues and those that are associations of all the governments in an area, and serve as important clearinghouses (traditionally called COGs—Council of Governments).

Regional governmental agencies dealing with specific policy issues exist to ensure that a broader, regional vision and perspective are achieved for issues that reach across local boundaries. Some of the issues that require regional perspectives, since their impacts reach across sometimes artificial boundaries of cities and counties, are water supply and usage, transportation, and environmental or pollution problems.

Examples of these types of regional agencies in California include the Bay Area Rapid Transit (BART) District and the Bay Area Air Pollution Control District. Like most regional agencies, an elected board of directors from all the counties comprising the district governs BART. It is funded through a combination of federal grants, state revenues and sales taxes in the applicable counties. The Bay Area Air Pollution Control District is an example of an issue that traverses city and county boundaries resulting in the need for significant intergovernmental relations and cooperation. Federal and state grant funding requiring oversight and accountability in an intergovernmental relations environment encourages such cooperation.

The voluntary associations of local governments are designed to facilitate resolution of regional problems (e.g., integration of various mass transit agencies) through cooperation, sharing of solutions, and serving as a clearinghouse for information. These councils of governments were very important in the 1960s and 1970s but have declined in importance in recent years—mainly with the decline of federal financial support. Today, those COGs that still exist are in search of missions that can help them pay for themselves. Examples include the Southern California Association of Governments (SCAG) and the Association of Bay Area Governments (ABAG). For instance, ABAG has created important roles for itself in serving as a clearinghouse for earthquake and other emergency related information and an important source of information for maps with estimates of potential earthquake damage. More recently, they have served as the facilitator and technical experts in assisting Bay Area governments to achieve a meaningful presence on the World Wide Web.

Redevelopment Agencies

There are 400 redevelopment agencies in California today. Their mission, outlined by the California Community Development Act, is to revitalize deteriorating areas by removing old, blighted housing typically located in older commercial and residential areas, develop new housing units (including affordable housing), and encourage neighborhood revitalization. These agencies have the authority to collect property taxes in order to develop housing. There is some accountability by the state, as these agencies have to report each year on the use of these funds to the California Housing and Community Development Agency.

Joint Exercise of Powers Act—
Working Together Via Contracts

In California, as in many states, there is a Joint Exercise of Powers Act that allows two agencies, internal or external, to work together and exercise joint powers to accomplish mutual goals. These goals can include sharing costs and reducing duplication of services but could also include a relationship that is more like contracting out for services. Examples include the Peninsula Joint Powers Board, the administrative agency for the San Francisco Peninsula Caltrain commuter service, the Southern California Regional Rail Authority, an agreement between the cities of Larkspur and Corte Madera to provide police services, an arrangement between five counties (Alpine, Amador, Calaveras, Mariposa, and Stanislaus) to provide emergency medical services, and an agreement between Yolo County and several cities to preserve Swainson's hawk foraging habitat. Actually, Caltrain is even a more complicated arrangement since the train conductors are federal Amtrak employees.

CONCLUSIONS

The world of local government units in California is exceedingly complex. Composed of many different and overlapping jurisdictions sometimes competing with one another for resources and business development, the intergovernmental relations are constantly changing and adapting. These circumstances make it even more difficult for everyday citizens to understand this world and its impact upon their lives—which is considerable. As former Speaker of the

U.S. House of Representatives Thomas P. "Tip" O'Neill frequently stated, "All politics is local." What happens at the local level is immensely important to us all—and we all need to take an interest in the politics and policy issues emerging there. Students and other citizens should strive to stay informed—follow what is happening in your communities—and get involved.

ADDITIONAL RESOURCES

California League of Cities. http://www.cacities.org.

California State Association of Counties. http://www.csac.counties.org/index.html.

U.S. Advisory Commission on Intergovernmental Relations. http://www.library.unt.edu/gpo/ACIR/Default.html.

NOTES

1. California League of Cities. 2000. Principles for Smart Growth. California League of Cities. Available at http://www.cacities.org/doc.asp?intParentID=1072&strPageType=doc.

2. Deil S. Wright. *Understanding Intergovernmental Relations,* 3rd ed. (Harcourt Brace & Co., 1988, updated by author in 1995).

3. Legislative Analyst's Office. 2000. 2000 CAL-Fact State-Local Finances Legislative Analyst Office.

4. Ibid.

5. As many as five cities in California may provide some health care service. Berkeley is the most outstanding example because of the broad spectrum of public health services it provides, the models it has established in public-private partnerships in its provision of such services, and the awards, honors, and praise it has received in recognition of the success of such endeavors.

6. Students interested in cutting-edge program administration are encouraged to research the rich body of work emerging in the wake of state implementation of the Temporary Assistance for Needy Families (TANF) welfare reform block grants resulting from the 1996 federal reform legislation. Welfare as an entitlement was ended. States are now given block grants with guidelines and some set parameters

but are free to experiment with "ending welfare as we know it." California combined its previous Aid to Families With Dependent Children (AFDC) and GAIN (workfare and job training) into CAL-WORKS. The October 1997 California Journal has an excellent article by John Borland, "Can Welfare Work?," on this subject. In addition, studies by the Public Policy Institute of California and data from the state Department of Social Services on San Mateo County provide a sober and an optimistic analysis of the success of CALWORKS to date as well as an examination of the program administration flexibility in TANF-CALWORKS. Needless to say, this is an exciting area of IGR.

7. Students seeking current information should refer to the latest available year of the California Government Code, Title 8: General Provisions, State Financing Provisions, Municipal and Superior and Consolidated Municipal/Superior Courts sections of the code. In addition, another excellent and current resource to understanding the myriad changes and their current status is the latest available Governors Budget Summary.

8. Campaign for Tobacco-Free Kids, American Cancer Society, American Heart Association, and American Lung Association. 2002. Show Us the Money:

An Update on the States' Allocation of the Tobacco Settlement Dollars. January 15, 2002: Available at http://tobaccofreekids .org/reports/settlements/2002/fullreport .pdf.

9. G. Block and Charles M. Price, eds., *California Government & Politics Annual, 1998–1999* (Sacramento, CA: Journal Press, 1998), 70.

10. Vincent Ostrom, Robert Bish, and Elinor Ostrom, *Local Governments in the United States* (San Francisco: Institute of Contemporary Studies, 1988), 182–187.

Index

About the Authors

Lawrence G. Brewster
Dean of the College of Professional Studies and interim dean of the School of Education at the University of San Francisco. Before joining USF, he was academic dean at Menlo College, and prior to that, he was dean of the School of Liberal Studies and Public Affairs at Golden Gate University. He was professor of political science and associate dean at San Jose State University. Dr. Brewster regularly consults in public policy and organizational development and has industry experience as former director of market research for BT Tymnet, an international data communications company. He is the author of several journal articles and books.

Genie N. L. Stowers
Professor and director of the Public Administration Program at San Francisco State University. She received the Ph.D. in political science and public policy from Florida State University in 1987. Professor Stowers teaches public policy, public budgeting, information management, digital government, and general public administration courses. She has published widely in the area of e-government and information management. Before service in academia, she worked in spousal-abuse shelters/rape crisis centers at the U.S. Department of Housing and Urban Development and for the state of Florida.